THE
BUSINESS
OF YOGA

THE
BUSINESS
OF YOGA

A STEP-BY-STEP GUIDE FOR MARKETING AND MAXIMIZING PROFITS FOR YOGA STUDIOS AND INSTRUCTORS

**Casey Conrad &
Howard VanEs, E-RYT500**

The Business of Yoga
A Step-by-Step Guide Marketing and Maximizing Profits for
Yoga Studios and Instructors

Published by:
Let'sDoYoga.com

ISBN: 978-0692256411

TABLE OF CONTENTS

INTRODUCTION

I remember the day I met my co-author, Howard VanEs, like it was yesterday. It was April, 1992. I was a young consultant in the health and fitness industry trying to make my way onto the international speaking stage. The path to getting there was to first establish a strong regional presence. I was doing just that by giving a workshop on Neuro Linguistic Programming (NLP) in membership sales through the New England Health, Racquet & Sportsclub Association (NEHRSA). The seminar was being hosted at a club in Wallingford, CT called Healthworks. I happened to be in the GM's office prior to the start of the seminar when Howard arrived. He was doing the ad design for the club.

Howard was the president and founder of an award winning ad group. He and I established instant rapport when he heard the seminar topic because he, himself, was a long-time NLP practitioner. We exchanged cards and later learned we had much more than NLP in common.

I engaged Howard's company to design the cover of what was to be my first sales and marketing book entitled *Selling Fitness; the complete guide to selling health club memberships.* This was the start of a life-long friendship and several business ventures together.

Later, an economic and personal health crisis brought Howard to attend a workshop at Kripalu Yoga & Retreat Center in Lennox, MA. His high praises for the facility led me to follow in his footsteps and so began our own individual journeys into the world of Yoga.

Seeking a "Life shift" in search for more fulfilling work, Howard closed down his ad agency, packed as many belongings into his car as was possible, and he and his dog Murphy headed to California to pursue a Master's Degree in Expressive Arts Therapy. It was during his second year in graduate school that Howard got his yoga teaching certification through Mt. Modonna Center in Watsonville, CA. And, as is the case with many things in life, after attaining his degree his passion for yoga outweighed his interest in becoming a therapist.

Over the years that followed, Howard taught yoga at many health clubs, local recreational centers and yoga studios. During our regular phone conversations he would constantly mention to me two things in particular: First, the growth of mainstream yoga was immense, which led him to write his first book, *Beginning Yoga: A practice manual.* Second his witnessing the struggle that most yoga teachers' and facilities had in growing and maintaining their studio and/or clientele. Of course, his background in advertising and marketing gave Howard a distinct advantage in growing his own classes and customer base.

While Howard was on his journey I was on my own. My speaking and consulting business had grown over 1,000% since the launch of my Selling Fitness book, which was translated into multiple languages. I grew the company and produced dozens of sales and marketing materials specific for health club operators—some of which Howard and I created and produced together.

Unlike Howard, my yoga life consisted of an annual one weekend trip out to Kripalu and the occasional class while visiting him in California. My travel and "type A" personality simply was not embracing a regular yoga practice. All that changed, however, when a nagging back problem turned chronic. It was then that I tried out many different forms of yoga, ultimately falling in love with a hot, vinyassa flow.

As each year passed Howard and I would constantly say, "We need to combine our expertise and do something that will help yoga teachers and studio owners build a more successful— stable—business." After years of discussion we are glad to say we finally have done it!

Why now, you ask? A lot of reasons, but one big one is that with the popularity of yoga reaching all-time highs, more and more "yoga entrepreneurs" are struggling. This pains us. And because we are both passionate advocates of yoga and serial entrepreneurs ourselves, we felt compelled to finally put words to paper and bring this important information to you.

We have organized this book in a way that allows you to either read it from cover to cover or take each chapter individually. Our goal with the material is simple: provide you with step-by-step instructions of how to build a profitable yoga business.

We start with a general understanding of the three ways to grow revenue in any business and discuss them as it relates to a yoga practice.

Next, we outline for you how to create a marketing plan and provide you with very specific strategies in the most popular and pertinent marketing categories as it relates to a yoga business. This will include traditional marketing, internet marketing and social media marketing—all of which are necessary in today's competitive marketplace.

We then turn our attention to discovering ways to generate more revenue from existing customers with creative packaging and product and service offerings.

Of course, no business book would be complete if we didn't discuss the process of selling. In this book we will focus on the general sales process and how your business can ensure they don't get a bad name as it relates to the customer sales experience.

Next we will discuss an extremely important aspect of a successful yoga business, which is client retention. In this section we will provide you with lots of ideas and strategies on how to keep your students happy, long-time attendees at your class or studio.

Finally, we will spend some time discussing KPI's, which stands for key performance indicators. The reality is that business is a numbers game and when you know what numbers (KPI's) to track and watch, you will ultimately make better business decisions.

Whether you are brand new to the business of yoga or a seasoned veteran, whether you actually own a yoga studio or are simply trying to grow your own class following, you'll find this book is packed with many great ideas and insights that will ultimately help you maximize your profits and success in your venture, no matter how big or small it may be.

Great care has been taken to provide you with a thorough overview of yoga marketing and for some this may be overwhelming, especially if you are new to this subject. While we recommend that you read over the entire book, you might find the implementation of the information presented easiest when you take one chapter at a time. We also suggest that many of the techniques and ideas offered can be effectively implemented through the use of an administrative or virtual assistant.

In good health,
Casey Conrad & Howard VanEs

CHAPTER 1

STANDING THE BUSINESS OF YOGA ON ITS HEAD

Most people who end up teaching yoga or owning a studio do so because they want to share their love of yoga and its many benefits with others. Few go into the business of yoga realizing they need a solid business or marketing plan.

This is not surprising for three reasons. First, yoga teacher programs are woefully inadequate at teaching teachers how to market their practice. Even credentialed programs usually don't offer more than an hour or two of marketing instruction.

Secondly, many yogis have taken on the idea that in order to be a good yoga teacher it means they are not allowed to enjoy financial success and all that it brings. If this describes you, you're happy and your life works like this, then we say "good for you." Unfortunately though, for many, this mindset results in so much austerity that having a yoga business becomes a financial struggle both personally and professionally. This doesn't serve you or your students. Make no mistake though, in order to be in business, you need students and a healthy cash flow. You need this to take care of yourself, your practice and your facility. If you are busy worrying about where the money to pay your rent is going to come from, then you will not be able to focus on what you do best – which is running your studio and/or teaching students.

> " *What would it be like for you to have enough money to create the studio of your dreams...*

If you believe that being a modern yogi means that you must be austere and can't enjoy financial well-being then we suggest that you consider the idea that the flip side of austerity is abundance. What would it be like for you to have enough money to create the studio of your dreams; to have the security of a financial cushion; to go to training programs; to attract top teachers to your studio; to save money for your retirement, and; to pay for healthcare? We believe that money in the hands of good people, with good intentions, can do good things. With this belief it is possible to have the best of both worlds—i.e. making a difference through yoga and enjoying abundance.

The third reason why teachers or studio owners don't have a marketing plan is because they just didn't know they needed one! If you have never run a successful business before then you probably don't recognize the great importance of marketing. This is true for those who go into any type of business. Marketing is the lifeblood of business!

The great news is that none of the above can stop you from having a successful yoga business if you truly want one. Within the pages of this book you will find everything you need to market your yoga business well. Let's get started!

CHAPTER 2

THE 3 WAYS TO GROW ANY BUSINESS

Whether you have a small business or large business; whether you sell widgets or yoga classes, there is one common denominator to any type of business; the fundamental ways of generating revenue. There are only three basic methods:

1. Get more customers.

2. Get customers to make bigger purchases.

3. Get customers to buy more frequently.

Of course, there are huge variations in how different types of businesses will go about utilizing each of these fundamental growth principles. A local hardware store is going to use different advertising and marketing tactics than the local hair salon, but the basics of business are the same no matter what industry, product or service. Because these concepts are so fundamental to your overall business success, let's talk about how each of these marketing principles can help maximize revenue and increase your profits.

INCREASING THE NUMBER OF CUSTOMERS

Anytime you do something that tries to attract new students you are utilizing the first component of business success. For any business to succeed it needs an ongoing source of new customers, so focusing on this is critical. Although particularly true in the early stages of a business, attaining new customers is a constant and necessary practice. Because of its importance, much of this book is dedicated to teaching you various marketing strategies that will help you attract new students.

> " *Discounting may boost sales in the short-term, but the long-term results can be devastating...*

Unfortunately, in a quest to bring in new students, many studios believe they need to lower their prices or offer deep multi-class discount cards. Discounting may boost sales in the short-term, but the long-term results can be devastating because you establish a lower perceived value in the minds of customers.

There are ways to entice prospects to buy without having to discount. For example, you can increase the perceived value of your offering by bundling other services or even products into packages. We will discuss this in greater detail when we get into the specific marketing strategies. For now just know that creativity in your marketing to new customers can create exceptional results that are not related to discounting. Not discounting leads to higher margins/profits—one of the two fundamental numbers you must focus on.

There are countless ways that you can attract new customers. Some require more money while others are virtually free. Here are a few tried and proven methods:

- Newspaper advertising in small local publications

- Flyer distribution to local businesses

- Small, targeted direct mail campaigns

- Google Adwords

- Facebook ads

- Networking with other local businesses

- Cross promotions with businesses that have similar customer bases

- Passing out business cards at a local Chamber event

- Setting up a promotional table at a local fair or show

- Providing free class pass donations to a local charity auction or raffle

- Promoting through your Facebook account or page

- Pro-actively asking current customers for referrals

These are just some of the most obvious and common marketing ideas. A good portion of this book will focus on these and other simple ways to attract new customers specifically for a yoga studio or practice. It is important, however, to note that adding more customers is only one of the three ways to grow profits—AND IT IS THE MOST EXPENSIVE.

That's correct, getting new customers is both the hardest and the most expensive way to generate profits yet it is the one area that most business owners put the majority of their attention. Why? Because it is the most obvious way to generate revenue.

Top businesses, however, recognize that they MUST utilize all three ways of revenue generation if they are to maximize long-term success. So, let's discuss those two other ways.

INCREASING THE SIZE OF A CUSTOMER'S PURCHASE

The second way to add profits to your bottom line is by increasing the size of your student's purchases. To tap into this concept, ask yourself, 'Without any additional marketing expenses, what else can I offer to students that would result in more revenue? What else do they need?'

Many people falsely assume that the easiest way to do this is by selling more expensive items or a larger amount. Those are certainly two ways to accomplish a larger purchase and in business they are commonly referred to as "up-sells." Upsells, however, are not the only ways, nor are they always the best with some buyers.

Think about it; with a yoga class you have a finite number of spots. If your classes are empty then it might make sense to run a short promotion where a discount is given on classes simply as a way to get bodies onto mats. But if your classes are fairly full and you use a discounting strategy to get a larger point of sale purchase then you have basically filled that mat spot at a lesser amount than you would have gotten. In our final chapter on Key Performance Indicators we will discuss the process of evaluating these types of decisions. Suffice it to say for now that you must recognize that there are multiple ways to increase a customer's purchase that don't involve discounting.

> *... an often overlooked yet highly successful strategy is the cross-sell.*

With services like yoga classes, an often overlooked yet highly successful strategy is the cross-sell. Here, instead of trying to get the customer to buy a larger number of classes the focus would be on getting them to buy related products or services. For example, yoga accessories like mats, blocks, or straps might be something you offer. Books or DVD's for when they cannot make it to a class are often overlooked but can be a wonderful edition—even when they aren't your own.

We know of a personal trainer who only did in-home visits and travelled around in a van that was outfitted to be a fitness store on wheels. Immediately after working with a new client (at their home), he would give them a coupon good for 20% off their entire purchase that day. After their initial workout, he took them out to the van, opened the doors and let them go shopping. The average spend was in excess of $200. Knowing that retail is typically a 100% markup he was still making plenty of money even after the 20% discount. Perhaps more importantly he was getting the client more emotionally engaged in their new lifestyle, which could have a positive impact on the length of time they remain a client.

Although this was not a specific yoga example, it perfectly exemplifies creativity in increasing the size of a customer's purchase. We hope it sparks some different ideas for you. Here are some other ways to consider increasing the size of a customer's purchase:

- Adding private lessons to your offering

- Selling branded apparel with your company name/logo

- Selling related ancillary products and services like meditation CD's, Aromatherapy items, sports beverages, water bottles and yoga clothing

- Selling workshops or special trainings

INCREASING THE FREQUENCY OF A PURCHASE

The third way to add profits to your bottom-line is by increasing the frequency of a customer's purchase. For most yoga studios and classes this means getting a customer to increase the number of times per week that they attend. That may sound so simple and obvious that you dismiss the thought, but we want you to stop and focus on the numbers as a way of seeing the power of this strategy.

Let's say you have a customer who attends one class per week on a Saturday. Your drop in rate is $15 per class. Assuming that with vacations and normal life interruptions this person participates 46 weeks out of the year, this one customer represents $690 in annual gross revenue from their class participation. Imagine if you could educate and motivate this person to move from one to two classes per week? You would double your income without ANY additional expenses! This is the power of increasing the frequency of purchases yet 99.9% of yoga studios and instructors do not put any time or attention onto this strategy. It is a pity because it is actually the easiest way to increase revenue.

There is no question that with yoga studios increasing the frequency of visits requires some creativity, but it will prove to be both profitable and rewarding. Any yoga teacher knows that when a student begins to really develop a "practice" they have significant physical and emotional breakthroughs. As you go through this book we encourage you to search for new and different ways to influence the frequency of visits with your students. Below are some basic ways to consider.

- Develop a frequent practitioner's program

- Run short term "program" series that focus on a specific outcome, benefit or theme

- Provide students with education on value of more frequent yoga

Very often your students will ask you how many times a week they should practice and this is an easy opportunity to suggest what you think is appropriate for them. Other times there are students that come just once a week who could benefit greatly by attending classes more frequently. We encourage you to give these people your guidance and share with them the type of benefits you think they might experience by coming more often.

WHERE TO FOCUS YOUR EFFORTS?

When teaching this information in our live seminars we will often get attendees asking, "Which of the three ways to grow business should I spend most of my time on?" Of course, that is a loaded question. The true answer is, "All three!" As we mentioned earlier, new businesses must focus on attaining new customers because without that they will surely go out of business. However, if from opening day a business also focuses on increasing the size of every customer's purchase <u>and</u> how to get customers to buy more often they will accelerate their profitability immensely. You see, when a business focuses on all three of these elements the progression of profits is exponential. Let us illustrate this further.

EXPONENTIAL RESULTS

We've all heard the expression "exponential," most likely in math class when our teacher had us do a simple calculation. 2 x 2 = 4, x 2 = 8, x 2 = 16, x 2 = 32. Each time the next number is multiplied by 2 it gets substantially bigger. That is rather straight forward and simple to understand.

In technical terms, exponential growth occurs when the amount being added to anything is proportional to the amount that's already there. Therefore, the bigger something is to begin with, the greater the resulting increase. In financial terms this is referred to as runaway expansion. To demonstrate, let's use an example.

Suppose that you have 50 students that attend an average of one class per week at $15 per class. Keeping the math simple at 4 weeks per month, this means you have total monthly revenue of $3,000. In addition, during the year, each of those students makes an average of $25 in ancillary purchases (drinks, books, straps, etc.). Keep in mind that not every student will make additional purchases so this is an average simply to provide this example. Financially, your revenue from this example would look like this:

50 students x 4 visits per month = 200 total class visits

200 total class visits X $15 per class = $3,000 per month in class revenue

Class revenue: $3,000/mo. X 12 months = $36,000 per year

Ancillary sales: $25 X 50 students = $1,250 per year

Total revenue: = $37,250 per year

Now imagine that through your marketing and sales efforts, you can improve your overall performance by just 10%. Many people make the mistake of thinking that a ten percent improvement means $3,725 in revenue. But that would be true only if making the calculation with simple arithmetic. In reality, each increase has an impact on the others. Therefore, when you improve each one of the categories, your end result is actually exponential!

Returning to our previous example, a 10% increase would mean 55 students per month, with ancillary sales of $27.50 per year. FURTHER, if we could improve the attendance by 10 percent that would mean every student would attend 4.4 times per month. With those numbers the calculations would be as follows:

55 students x 4.4 visits per month = 242 total class visits

242 total class visits X $15 per class = $3,630 per month in class revenue

Class revenue: $3,630/mo. X 12 months = $43,560 per year

Ancillary sales: $27.5 X 55 students = $1,375 per year

Total revenue: = $44,935 per year

THE MATH IS COMPELLING

Though this is a very simple example, light bulbs should be going off in your head! Do the calculation, and you'll see that a 10% improvement in all three revenue generating areas results in an actual, exponential 20.6% improvement in overall revenue. This shows why it's so important to generate improvements in all three areas of revenue generation.

The exciting part is that these incremental improvements are all totally within your reach. Most businesses focus only on gaining new customers AND they aren't maximizing their marketing opportunities. Even for highly successful businesses, some marketing opportunities always remain untapped—especially in regard to increasing ancillary sales and the frequency of purchases.

The remainder of this book is going to help you realize your full marketing potential! We are going to first show you how to attract more customers, which is always the first step. Then, throughout our discussions we will provide you with strategies for increasing the size of your students' purchases as well as getting them to buy more often. Taken together you will find multiple ways to maximize your revenue generation abilities and profits. So, let's get into the marketing.

CHAPTER 3

THE POWER OF THE MARKETING PARTHENON

A Parthenon is an ancient Greek temple whose triangular shaped pediment is supported with a number of pillars. The more pillars any such structure has, the stronger it will be.

Jay Abraham was the first marketing guru to use the image of the Parthenon as a simple analogy: Your marketing strength and ultimate success in business depends on how many "pillars" you have to support your business. A pillar is a marketing tactic.

If you only have two ways—aka "pillars"—to attract new customers and one of them fails, your financial roof will fall in. However, if you have ten pillars or more, even if several of them fail, the risk of failure is greatly minimized.

> " *By distributing your marketing expectations across many different supports, you will achieve greater stability...*

At one time or another, most business owners have been guilty of putting too much faith into one campaign, ad or effort and then later, having to scramble to pay that's month's bills. For yoga studios and instructors—who typically don't have any business background—the failure to utilize multiple marketing efforts is all too common. By distributing your marketing expectations across many different supports, you will achieve greater stability—hence, less risk.

Instructors trying to build their own class size might be reading this and think, "This chapter's information doesn't apply to me."

Not true; regardless of the size or scope of any business, the concept of the Parthenon can be applied. When you think about it, that statement makes sense. The more ways in which you market yourself or your business the greater the number of prospect sources you will generate, hence potential customers.

When applying Abraham's Parthenon concept to the marketing of yoga studios there are six primary pillars: External, Internal, Guerrilla, Corporate, Community and Retention. As you'll learn, each pillar has numerous possible sub-pillars. Let's first define each of these pillars and understand how they support and strengthen one another. In later chapters we will discuss which pillars are most appropriate to the marketing of a yoga studio or practice and provide details on each of those concepts.

EXTERNAL MARKETING

External marketing refers to any effort that reaches a large number of people in your marketplace. For yoga studios, the most common would be ads in local newspapers, inserts, direct mail, flyers, buying an email list, banner ads, Google AdWords and Facebook ads. Obviously some of those are more traditional marketing efforts and the latter few are internet based.

Though external marketing efforts are expensive and their response rates have dropped off considerably, they remain a necessity for most startup businesses. For one thing, external marketing reaches lots of people in your local market. Second, even if they don't draw high rates of response, it's sometimes important to create brand awareness, or what is referred to as Top of Mind Awareness. When you are new in any community, TOMA is particularly critical.

Finally, external marketing helps to establish and bolster credibility. When consumers see advertisements repeatedly, they're more likely to assume your business is solid and thriving. Though a "false association," this psychological factor can justify your decision to spend big on external advertising. Certainly many yoga studios have smaller marketing budgets, making many of the external efforts unavailable, but there will be situations and instances where external marketing is both advantageous and economically viable.

INTERNAL MARKETING

Internal marketing refers to marketing efforts you conduct inside your facility or to smaller mailings that you generate using your own databases. Referral programs and campaigns, promotions to former or inactive students, or specials on other products and services you offer are all common examples of internal marketing efforts.

Many people confuse external and internal marketing because there is some overlap. The primary difference is scope and size. External marketing attempts to reach the masses where internal marketing reaches smaller, niche groups through self-generated mailing lists and member referrals.

GUERRILLA MARKETING

The term guerrilla marketing was coined by the famous author Jay Conrad Levinson (no relationship to the Conrad in this book). Levinson has published a series of fabulous books for salespeople and small businesses, offering hundreds of low-cost marketing ideas. Another term for guerrilla marketing is "grass roots" marketing because typically these efforts are done the old fashioned way—by putting your sneakers on and going out and interacting with potential customers and other business operators.

> Another term for guerrilla marketing is "grass roots" marketing...

There is an endless number of guerrilla marketing ideas but one thing they all have in common is being no or low cost. This is very appealing to small businesses.

For a yoga studio owner or instructor the biggest challenge with guerrilla marketing isn't the ideas but rather finding the time. All guerrilla marketing efforts take time to establish and maintain. Finding the proper mix between ideas that are less time consuming and others that are very labor intensive will be the key to maintaining this pillar. For example, compare dropping promotional materials off at the coffee shop you visit each morning with setting up a table at the local health food store. The former is quite simple while the latter will require much more of your time.

Some of the more common guerrilla marketing strategies ideal for promoting yoga classes include flyer distributions, tri-fold brochure stands (also called Take-One's), door hangers (not just for doors, but what they are called), and business cards.

One important aspect of guerrilla marketing is called joint marketing or reciprocal marketing with other local businesses. In return for another business owner's help in promoting your studio or classes to their customers, you, in turn, provide exposure for that business to your students. Establishing a handful of these partnerships is simple, fun and can be highly effective. Furthermore, websites make it easy to leverage guerrilla marketing efforts by creating online partnership coupon programs that literally cost nothing (except time) to establish. A few natural businesses for yoga studios to partner with include massage therapists, chiropractors, nutritionists and health food stores, just to name a few.

COMMUNITY MARKETING

Community marketing, sometimes referred to as community outreach, refers to everything you do that builds goodwill in the community. Like guerrilla marketing, there are endless ways to do community marketing. Some of the more common include sponsoring a local sports team, hosting a blood drive, organizing students to participate in a local charity event, volunteering at road races and sporting events, and collecting donations for organizations like Toys for Tots or the local food bank.

One important but often overlooked element of community marketing is sending out press releases on a regular basis. Because press release services report to all the internet search engines, they can be a particularly powerful way to create brand awareness and loyalty. Press releases can contain news about you, your studio or events taking place at your studio.

> *...your goal is to show that you're an active participant in your community...*

One important distinction about community marketing is that these efforts are not intended to immediately attain customers. Rather, your goal is to show that you're an active participant in your community, helping to create a feeling of trust and encouraging locals to "want" to do business with your company. Because of this, many small business operators don't do any community marketing. This is a big mistake because having exposure in your community and showing them you are an active participant who gives back can go a long way in winning their business. Therefore, even if it is on a small scale we encourage you to utilize this pillar of marketing.

CORPORATE MARKETING

As its name implies, corporate marketing refers to any activity where you market yourself to local businesses. Although it sounds similar, this is different than guerrilla marketing. Corporate marketing tries to engage the employees of a company whereas guerrilla marketing is gaining access to the customer base of that business.

Some common corporate marketing efforts would include on-site health fairs, posters in a lunchroom, fliers distributed on employees' desks or at a reception, and "Lunch & Learns," where you might provide a free on-site educational lecture or sample class during a lunchtime break. Stress management, back care, chair yoga and shoulder care are highly sought after subjects in the corporate setting.

For the purposes of this book we will not be focusing on corporate marketing because it is highly time consuming and most yoga studio owners and instructors won't be able to attain enough exposure or customers to make it worthwhile. This is NOT to say that corporate marketing isn't effective; just not what we will spend time on here.

RETENTION MARKETING

Retention marketing refers to anything you do to try and keep students coming to classes. Retention is always an issue with services like exercise classes. Certainly there always seems to be a core of students who are loyal followers through seasons, schedule changes and even moves, but there also seems to be an endless supply of people who disappear as quickly as they show up.

> *It is so much easier and less expensive to keep a customer than it is to find a new one!*

Studios and teachers who take the time to give retention marketing some serious effort will soon realize the power (and financial reward) of this pillar. It is so much easier and less expensive to keep a customer than it is to find a new one! This is such a powerful statement we are going to say it again. It is so much easier and less expensive to keep a customer than it is to find a new one! Best of all, because almost no yoga studios or teachers do anything in this area, you will quickly stand out with your students as someone who cares. Ultimately, the dividends you will earn from this will give you much more than financial returns.

There are many fun ways in which you can establish retention marketing. Parties, loyalty classes or gifts, internal attendance competitions, emailing to active as well as inactive students, or something as simple and ordinary as birthday cards are all inexpensive and effective. Really, any proactive attempt to keep students engaged and coming to class is part of your retention pillar. Making retention one of your six *primary* pillars keeps you from letting such efforts fall by the wayside.

THE POWER OF PILLARS

Earlier, you saw that the strength of a Greek temple results from multiple pillars: The more pillars, the greater the stability. That makes sense from a logical engineering standpoint, and it is easy to see the analogy to marketing. You can further strengthen your marketing effectiveness by using one or more strategies from each pillar, every single month of the year. Planning out all your marketing efforts months ahead of time, tracking the results and tweaking accordingly is what makes an effective marketing plan. Utilizing the marketing Parthenon approach with your plan greatly improves a business' success. A simple example will help make the point.

Imagine two yoga studios in the same locality, both with similar styles, class offerings and pricing. Both also have the same marketing budget. Studio #1 spends its entire budget on an aggressive direct mail campaign. However, studio #2 divides up its budget across multiple pillars. Some of that money goes into direct mailings, some to mailers to former students; some is applied toward referral gifts, and a cooperative event with two local businesses. The remaining budget is spent providing a bottled water station in a local outdoor hot weather event and mailing out a free class coupon to members whose birthdays fall during that month.

Let's take a hypothetical prospect: Jane Smith, who lives in the community where these studios are both located. In her mailbox one month, she finds a direct mail brochure from Studio #1. She's interested in losing a few pounds before summer, so she puts the mailer aside, intending to phone and make an appointment.

That very month, Jane gets a mailer from Studio #2, which she adds to the same pile of "intentions" where she left the first one. But in addition, Jane also gets an email from a friend of hers, a student at Studio #2, offering Jane a complimentary pass to a class. That week, ironically enough, Jane is picking up her dry cleaning when on the counter she sees a brochure from Studio #2 and the week after happens to notice the studio's free water booth at the local sports event.

Most likely, Studio #2 will have left a greater impression on Jane because she seems to notice their presence everywhere she turns. There's no guarantee that Jane will go visit Studio #2 instead of #1, since convenience and other factors will influence her decision. But Studio #2 has placed itself in a better position psychologically with Jane and everyone else. They may not be the better studio or the more financially stable, but from all appearances to the community, they seem to be spending more money, are more involved and therefore, are perceived more credible. All of those external "public relations" factors usually translate into more customers.

THE SYNERGISTIC EFFECT!

Any business that uses the multi-pillar approach gets not only the benefit of greater stability but together the pillars create a synergistic effect. One dictionary definition of synergy is, "Two or more agents or forces interacting so that their combined effect is greater than the sum of their separate individual efforts." The more pillars you utilize for your marketing efforts, the greater your overall response rates and Top of Mind Awareness will be. Ultimately, TOMA means more customers. This synergistic effect is exactly what our example illustrated, with Studio #1 using only one pillar, but Studio #2 using multiple pillars. They both had the exact same marketing budget, but Studio #2 spent that money to generate more awareness, more credibility and most likely, more sales.

Two important points to emphasize here; one, your business must incorporate multiple pillars in its marketing mix. Two, within each pillar, you should identify and utilize various marketing efforts to create additional strength and stability. To stick to our Parthenon analogy, one pillar would be made of poured concrete, while the second one would also be of concrete, but poured over multiple rods of steel all welded together. Obviously, our second pillar will be stronger.

THE MARKETING PLAN

We have all heard the adage, "If you fail to plan you plan to fail." This obviously applies more than ever to the marketing of a business. A business can't simply open its doors and expect customers to find it. "If you build it they will come" only happened in the movies! Therefore, it is important to answer these questions:

- Do you have an annual marketing plan? (That means 6-12 months, planned out.)

  ❏ Yes ❏ No

- If you plugged all your existing marketing efforts into the Parthenon model, are you doing one or more activities in <u>at least three</u> pillars every single month?

  ❏ Yes ❏ No

- Do you put enough effort into each individual pillar to ensure that each is strong—every month of the year?

  ❏ Yes ❏ No

- If you wanted to sell your business or practice tomorrow, is your marketing plan written out in a format clear enough that the new owner/person could step right in and follow that plan without any confusion?

  ❏ Yes ❏ No

If you answer no to any of those questions, I suggest you take the time to create a marketing plan. This means that you grid out the following things for each and every month of the year:

1. Exactly what you are going to do in the various pillars. This needs to be very specific. Therefore, saying "Local newspaper ad" is NOT a plan. Rather, 3 x 5 add in X paper on the 1st and 3rd Tuesday of the month. Further, note the theme, and the offer. So, if it is September in North America you might say, "Back to School, free two-day class pass." Of course, you will still need to eventually create the ad copy, have it laid out and approved, but at least knowing what you are going to do will give you a clear direction. Please download the marketing grid handout to help make this process easier.

2. Outline all costs associated with that marketing effort (on the grid). So, sticking with our earlier ad example, it might cost $200 per circulation for a total of $400 (small, local paper). This is a simple way to be overseeing your monthly marketing budget during the planning phase.

3. Get a large 3-ring binder, a set of January – December tabs, and a packet of clear 3-hole sheet protectors. For every single marketing effort you do in any month, place a copy of the ad, letter, flier, etc. into one of the sheet protectors. This allows you to keep a good record of what you have done and gives you easy, organized access to samples when you need to do another piece.

4. At the end of each month, use the marketing tracker sheet provided as a download at the end of this chapter to calculate the return on investment from each marketing activity.

5. Organize binders by calendar year and label accordingly. When planning the next calendar year you now have resources to refer to and actual outcomes to help make better decisions about your next year's marketing plan.

CHAPTER 4
TRADITIONAL MARKETING

With an understanding of the marketing Parthenon strategy, now let's get into the specific tactics that you should consider utilizing in your marketing plan. This chapter will focus on the more traditional marketing efforts and leave all the internet strategies and tactics to future chapters. The primary focus will be on external, internal and guerrilla marketing strategies. We will end with a short section on community efforts. A later chapter will be entirely dedicated to retention marketing.

EXTERNAL MARKETING

Remember that external marketing is very traditional; things like newspaper ads and inserts, coupon programs and direct mailers. Of course, all of these efforts require a more substantial cash outlay than many of the other marketing efforts that we will discuss later. In marketing, however, do not confuse cash outlay with being "expensive" because it is all relative.

If your business spent $2,000 on an ad but attracted 100 new customers that spent just $30 each, then the ad would more than pay for itself. Therefore, when deciding whether or not some kind of newspaper ad should be included in your marketing plan you must know the costs, the potential exposure to qualified prospects, and a reasonable guestimate of how many new customers you might derive from the effort.

NEWSPAPER ADS

For many yoga studios or instructors growing their own classes in rented space, newspaper ads in smaller, local papers can be an option. Unfortunately, if you are trying to build your business in a larger, metropolitan area, many newspapers won't be viable because the reach of the newspaper is vast and they charge accordingly, making it financially risky to try. With smaller newspapers, however, there are three different types of advertising that might work: display ads, classified ads and inserts. Let's discuss the pros and cons of each.

Display advertising is probably the most common for local businesses. This is when you have information in the newspaper that tries to get the attention of the reader. Display ads are typically sold in sizes such as, ¼ of a page, 1/8th of a page or by columns, which usually represent a certain number of total inches.

> *Many small businesses make the mistake of creating what are known as "Tombstone ads."*

Many small businesses make the mistake of creating what are known as "Tombstone ads." This refers to an ad where the business basically puts their name and logo at the top of the advertisement, has a short bullet point list of the products or services offered, and closes with the address, phone number and webpage information. Basically the ad does nothing more than let the reader know that the business is open (assuming the reader even notices the ad)! The reason this type of ad is referred to as "Tombstone" is two-fold. First, like the name of the deceased on a burial stone, the name of the business is at the top. The more important reason it is called Tombstone is because running this type of ad often leads to the death of a business. Let us explain.

In marketing every dollar must be utilized with the primary objective of getting new customers through the doors. Tombstone ads do nothing to really get the reader's attention nor do they create any motivation to buy. Look at the following two ads and notice how they are the same size, hence cost, but that one creates a much more compelling reason for the reader to call or visit.

NAMASTE
YOGA STUDIO

CLASSES FOR ALL LEVELS OF STUDENTS

7 DAYS A WEEK

DROP-IN'S WELCOME

12 MAIN STREET
ANYWHERE, USA
123-456-7891

Ineffective, "Tombstone" style ad doesn't have a call to action.

Free
Yoga Class

Yoga is a great way to improve
your health & get in shape

Classes for all levels of students
7 Days a week
Drop-in's welcome

For your free class coupon visit
www.NamasteYoga.com/FreeClass

12 Main Street

Anywhere, USA

123-456-7891

Effective ad design entices a customer to take action and opt-in.

Hopefully you can see the significant difference between these two. The one on the right should get more attention <u>and</u> a greater response. In the chapter, Playing by the Numbers, we will spend considerable time discussing how you must track certain numbers in order to make better business decisions. Your marketing response will be one of those KPI's (Key Performance Indicators). For now just know that with any type of ad you run—whether it is newspaper or otherwise—you want to avoid Tombstone style ads and focus on creating direct response ads that will pay for themselves with new customers. A good rule of thumb for all advertising is to be sure to make an offer. By doing so you will motivate the reader to take action and you will be able to measure results.

We realize that many of you reading this book might not be considering newspaper advertising and that's okay. Only you will ultimately know what is best for your business and your market-place. If, however, you are considering newspaper we want to give you some important insights and strategies to utilize.

- If you own a studio and newspaper is affordable, seriously consider using it during your grand opening. Not only will you reach much of the community but being in the paper adds a level of credibility in the consumer's mind. Furthermore, consistent newspaper ads offer an element of "social proof"—i.e. because you advertise regularly you must be doing okay, hence a trustworthy business. Of course, this might not be the case but it is how the consumer "sees" it.

- If you are just opening your studio you will quickly be visited by the newspapers ad representative. They will tell you they would like to do a story on you and then make it fairly clear that in order for that story to get any real attention you need to be a paying customer of the paper. Know that they will attempt to have you sign a long-term contract; don't do it; at least not until you have proven it will work for you. Even if it means they won't run the story we strongly suggest you follow this advice. Instead, negotiate a trial period with them, letting them know that before you will sign any contract you need to have enough data to see if the advertising will be effective.

- For the vast majority of readers who won't be doing display advertising on a regular basis, establish a relationship with your local representative to be notified of "dead space" or "remnant space" in any particular issue. This refers to space they have not sold or single columns that create a very weird space size that the paper usually fills with ads for themselves. Very often these types of spaces can be negotiated at deep discounts. It means you must be more creative with your ad design and be ready to provide it quickly to the paper, but it is worth the planning.

NEWSPAPER INSERTS

Inserts are a good option if you can't do traditional display advertising in the newspaper—either because it is cost prohibitive or because it doesn't make sense in your geographic area. Inserts are those pieces of paper that are inserted into the middle of your newspaper. Very often these will be 8 ½ x 11 sheets of paper or color post cards. Some smaller newspapers charge a small fee to put an insert into the paper and have you take care of all the printing. Some papers offer the complete package.

> " *One benefit of inserts is that they have a greater chance of being read.*

One benefit of inserts is that they have a greater chance of being read. Compare a display ad that is in the 3rd section of the paper on the 19th page with a bright orange insert that falls out when the paper is opened. The chances of someone seeing an insert is statistically greater than a display ad. Another benefit of inserts is that people tend to hold onto inserts where they often won't cut an ad out of the paper. They key to an insert is going to be finding a local newspaper that make this accessible to small business operators.

For those of you considering inserts, here are some tips.

- In geographic areas where the paper distribution is above 20,000, inquire as to whether or not that paper offers inserts by carrier route. Sometimes a paper will actually offer the ability to place an insert in only a certain zip code or zone area. This allows you to be very targeted around the area in which your studio or class is located.

- Be certain that your insert is a direct response ad—meaning that it is designed to either make the phone ring, drive the reader to a website for something free or get them to visit your studio or class. Do NOT spend the money on an insert simply to let people know your studio is open. That is a waste of money.

- When doing inserts, a business is often given the opportunity to spend more money and do a double sided printing. We have experienced absolutely no difference in response rates yet it will cost you more money. Therefore we suggest you stick to single sided inserts.

CLASSIFIED ADS

Many businesspeople are confused when we suggest they use classified ads to promote their business. Let's face it, typically the classifieds are utilized to sell things like cars, appliances and houses or promote business opportunities. True enough, but we have personal experience with several fitness studios that have successfully used classified ads to get new students. The reason why is because classified ads are incredibly cheap. Therefore, if a business obtains one new customer from a small classified ad it will pay for itself.

The question we are asked is "So, where exactly do I put the ad and what do I say?" Good questions. Some of your decision will depend upon the categories that your local newspaper offers but let's provide you with some common examples.

Most newspapers will have a section entitled "Community" where you can post upcoming events. Why not offer a free introduction to yoga class. If you are concerned about current students wanting a free class then simply put a disclaimer in the ad that it is for new students only. Think about focusing these intro classes towards specific populations; pregnant women, seniors, moms and babies, etc. Of course much of this will depend upon the style of yoga you are offering but obviously you can adjust accordingly.

Another classified area that you could put an ad in would be "Items for sale." Okay, so you don't have a physical item for sale but you are offering classes for sale. Why not put it in the sporting goods section? If the total cost is $24 for a couple of lines and you get even one taker it will pay for itself!

NEWSPAPER PERSPECTIVE

There is no doubt that the newspaper industry is dying. More and more papers go out of business every month as people move away from printed materials and more towards online news. BUT, until the paper in your area goes under, it could prove to be a viable marketing avenue for your studio or practice. You won't know until you identify options that are cash-flow affordable and you track and measure the response rates.

DIRECT MAIL

Direct mail refers to any type of mailer that is sent into homes in large numbers. In the United States there are typically three types of direct mail options that make sense for yoga studios. The first is a post card mailer, the second is a coupon pack, and the third is to be included in a group mailing put together by companies that specialize in doing this. Certainly you could do a letter mailer or even a brochure mailer but that is not typical because of the higher cost. Let's discuss the more popular modalities.

A post card mailer is exactly what it sounds like. Your business buys a list of prospects in the geographic area of your studio or practice and you send a post card directly to their home. Lists can be bought by zip code, or by investing more one can buy a list that has more "filters" like interest in fitness or even someone who subscribes to a particular magazine. The more number of filters the smaller the list will be but the more qualified it will be as well in addition to being more expensive.

With mailing list companies being very competitive (Infousa, Leadsplease, Onesource) and the ability to have post cards easily designed and printed through companies like VistaPrint and GotPrint, direct mailers are accessible to any size business. That said, we must warn you that direct mail seems to be having a lower and lower response rate since 2000. Certainly we are not saying "don't do direct mail," but rather are cautioning you to be intelligent about the size sample you try and accurately tracking and measuring response rates. (We will discuss the tracking and KPI's in a later chapter.) Be sure to use a motivational offer with an expiration date on all direct mail pieces. One way to improve your response rates from mailers is to utilize your own more qualified list. We will discuss this in the section on Internal Marketing.

Let's turn now to coupon packs, which refer to any type of mailing done through a company that places lots of coupons into an envelope that gets delivered to all the homes within a specific zip code region. In the United States the two most popular coupon mailing programs are ValPak and Money Mailer. Both of these are franchise programs that can be found in just about every single town.

Of course, as with any marketing medium there are mixed reviews with coupon programs. Some business operators swear by them while others get little or no response. Our experience is that if you live in a smaller town it can be an inexpensive way to reach lots of households. Further, given that the demographic of those who open coupon packs are women, you at least know that the coupon has a good chance of being seen by your target market. Certainly you would only utilize a coupon pack if your ad follows a direct response format, typically a free class trial or a very low entry level price that creates consumer action.

> *One final coupon type program that is available in many towns across the US is called Clipper Magazine.*

One final coupon type program that is available in many towns across the US is called Clipper Magazine. The same basic principle applies, just that instead of the coupon being part of an envelope it is delivered in a magazine format. One nice thing about the Clipper is that often there will be articles throughout the magazine that create more engagement and interaction with the reader. Although these articles are usually nothing more than paid for advertisements that are written to appear like an article, the result is that the magazine might stay around on the coffee table longer than a coupon pack on the counter. At the end of the day, you won't know if any of these options will work unless you try.

RADIO AND TELEVISION

For many studios and instructors the idea of using radio or television advertising is simply out of the question due to its wide geographical reach and the expense. However there are a couple situations where we believe it can be advantageous to use these media.

The first is if you have multiple studio locations within a defined geographical area. This makes sense because the cost of the media is shared among all your facilities. Secondly, your local cable company may offer television advertising that is targeted both geographically and demographically. The rates for this kind of advertising may fall within your budget and be worth testing. As with all media, be sure that you do a careful analysis of your break even before you purchase them; how many new students will you need in order to pay for this advertising?

A NECESSARY EVIL

We've talked about the most common forms of "traditional" external advertising utilized by yoga studios and instructors. For many of you, external advertising will not be the most effective medium but rather a necessary evil to gain market exposure and credibility—especially in the early days of business. Know that if external marketing is cost prohibitive in your area it simply means that you will have to depend upon the other marketing pillars to gain the exposure and marketing reach you need to succeed.

INTERNAL MARKETING

Unlike external marketing that is often done on a larger scale, internal marketing refers to efforts that you have greater control over and typically leverage your own database and customer relationships. The most important internal marketing tactics your yoga studio or practice will utilize are referral programs, letters to customers who inquired about classes, individuals who stopped by but never continued, mailings to former students, and in-house promotions on products and/or services you offer.

REFERRAL PROMOTIONS

Let's start with what could be the single most significant marketing tactic for your business; referrals. There are lots of reasons why referrals are so important. First, when a potential student hears good things about your studio or class from another they will be positively influenced by the recommendation. Second, customers who are referred by others need little or no "sales" influence. Third, if someone is referred by an existing student the relationship between them will have a positive impact on their consistent usage; people are more apt to stick with yoga or an exercise program if they have support. Finally, the customer acquisition cost (what it costs in marketing to get a new customer) is extremely low, if not nothing. For all of these reasons and probably many more, it is imperative that you incorporate referral programs into your business.

Before we get into discussing the various types of referral programs that you can utilize, let's first talk about referral strategy. There are many schools of thought as it relates to obtaining student referrals. On one end of the spectrum is "Customers will be so happy they will naturally tell people about us." The other end is "Provide the most financially advantageous incentives to encourage referrals." It will ultimately be your decision as to what type of referral strategy you want to take but we suggest you find a happy medium. This can be done by providing some incentive for people to refer, while generally encouraging customers to tell others about your business by letting them know you appreciate their spreading the good word. This type of approach will allow you to maximize referrals while maintaining a reasonable marketing cost for new students.

The next obvious question that we are asked is, "So, how much should I spend on incentives?" The answer is, "It depends." We aren't trying to be vague here but the reality is that to determine how much you should spend on a referral incentive you MUST know what the normal cost of acquiring a new student is and/or what the lifetime value of that student is. We will be discussing these KPI's in a later chapter but let's be certain you understand the basic concept here.

Suppose that you are currently spending $1,000 per month for your advertising and marketing efforts. As a result you are getting an average of 20 new students monthly. Although a very simple calculation, we can say that the basic marketing cost to obtain a new student is $50. If, through your tracking, you know that the average student comes to 20 classes before dropping out, and each class is $15, the lifetime value of that student (not including any other purchases for products or other services) would be $300. Knowing those figures, you can now make an intelligent— numbers-based—decision about how much to appropriate towards referral incentives.

At the end of that process you might be saying to yourself, "That is way too complicated and I don't want to think that much!" That's okay too. You might want to keep it really simple and say to your students, "If you refer someone and they purchase 5 or more classes, I will give you one free class pass." Ultimately every customer base is slightly different and we do not want to assume we understand your students. What we do understand is human nature, so let's end this strategy discussion by saying this:

> **Humans are more likely to refer others to your product or service if there is something in it for them.**

Humans are more likely to refer others to your product or service if there is something in it for them.

It is easy to get defensive and say, "We won't want to be like that; we want people to refer others because they want to, not because we bribed them to do it." But that isn't how the world goes around. Sure, we hope that your students love you and your yoga classes so much that they want to run around telling everyone but that rarely happens. At the very least you need to put a referral program in place so your students know that a) you want referrals, and; b) you appreciate their referrals—even if that appreciation comes in a form other than something with monetary value. The bottom line is that too many businesses assume that customers will simply give referrals.

Sadly they are wrong and many end up out of business because they did not find ways to encourage and boost referrals. So, with all that said, let's move on to discussing referral programs.

There are three different types of referral efforts that you should be utilizing; on-going, campaigns, and new student programs. On-going is exactly what it sounds like; establishing some kind of program where when a student refers another student something is triggered. Maybe it is something as simple as a $5 gift card towards classes or product purchases, maybe it is a free class coupon or perhaps you develop a more sophisticated points program where the member can accrue points for larger rewards. It might be that you simply send them a "Good Karma" thank you note with a personal message inside. You decide what you want to do, but make it a system so you are consistent.

Next are referral campaigns. This refers to a special promotion you might run in an effort to get a big surge in new students. For example, let's say that your studio wants to add some new classes to the schedule but in order to do that you have to get more bodies into the studio, not just spread the existing student base across more classes. Therefore you would consider putting together a campaign where, for a specific period of time you encourage students to refer others to the studio. There are entire books written on referral promotions so let us provide you with just a few examples to get your creative brain working on ideas for yourself.

T-SHIRT PROMO

People love to get branded T-shirts. This is especially true when it is for a place or product they love. Even if your business does not currently offer any branded clothing for sale, it is easy to have a couple of dozen T-shirts made at a very reasonable cost. Create a campaign whereby any student who refers a new student to the studio will be entered into a drawing at the end of the promotion to win a T-shirt. The more friends they refer the more chances they have of winning. This is a great promotion to run when you offer drop in classes because you do not know whether that new person will continue. If, on the other hand you actually sell packages of classes or sessions in time frames (12-week program with a specific start and end date), you could easily award the referring member a T-shirt once the new student joins.

Obviously, you can take the exact same concept as the T-shirt promotion and substitute any similarly valued item. For example: a yoga mat, bag or carrying strap, or perhaps a small workout towel. There are only two necessary "rules" to follow. First, that the item is desirable. The cooler the item, the more the customer will want to win it. Second, is that the item cannot be purchased in order to create scarcity. Therefore, if they really want the item they will figure out a way to generate a referral.

GET-AWAY

This campaign idea is a bit more involved but is also very exciting. The basic premise is to find a yoga retreat location within driving distance of your area. Either outright purchase a weekend package or, if you are able to, work out some kind of reduced price in exchange for advertising at your studio. Believe it or not, yoga retreat locations who know their target market are often very willing to offer other businesses a discount in exchange for being a sponsor on the advertising and promotional materials of the campaign.

Similar to the T-shirt concept, establish some criteria for referrals and how to gain an entry into the raffle. With a larger prize you may run the promotion for two or three months and have a minimum number of referrals. Another twist on this type of promotion is to have the winner be the person who referred the most new customers. Our experience with this, however, is that it de-motivates the majority of students after the first few weeks because once someone is in the lead others don't believe they can catch up and they just stop participating.

NON-MONETARY PRIZES

Some of you may be reading this and thinking to yourself, "I don't have the money or the time to go out and organize these types of referral programs." Relax and be creative. Why not offer private lessons or even something as unique as a private couple's yoga lesson followed by a candlelight dinner that you bring to their home. This assumes you can either cook or foot the bill for take out! The bottom line is that you are only limited by your own creativity.

The final type of referral we will discuss is new student referrals. As the name implies, this is a referral program that is specifically offered to new students. How are new student referrals different from on-going referrals or campaigns? It is just a matter of semantics; you are still trying to encourage referrals and are simply using this moment in time to create an opportunity to ask for referrals. Here's why.

Marketers know that the moment someone buys something there is a window of opportunity to obtain referrals. Think about it; when you first buy something you are so excited about the purchase that you often go tell numerous people. It's human nature so why not use that to your advantage? One simple way to accomplish this is to create a welcome packet for each new student. This could be a short fact sheet on the studio, (or you), a class schedule, an educational sheet for getting the most out of your yoga classes and voila, perhaps a couple of referral coupons that allow a friend to come to class for ½ price! You could also include a nice informational sheet about how individuals who practice yoga with friends are more likely to stick with their program than those that go it alone. Whether you offer coupons for discounts or not, the key is find creative ways to encourage new students to refer.

PASSES & PROMOTIONAL MATERIALS

We've now discussed three different types of referral programs; on-going, campaigns and new student. No matter which of these you utilize, it is important that you create the right tools that will support the program. The one tool that you must have is called a referral pass. Although there are many formats you can use, a referral pass must be professionally designed and printed, conveying the highest level of professionalism. The passes should have a place to write the guest's name, the referring student's name and a place where an expiration date can be written or stamped in.

> **The one tool that you must have is called a referral pass.**

The second tool that you should have is supporting promotional materials, like flyers and possibly posters, depending upon your situation. These materials are used to help inform the students about the promotion (especially campaigns) and can help to create excitement for the program.

Perhaps the most important tool, however, is you and your enthusiasm. Belief sells and if you convey to students the appreciation for referrals to your business and get them excited about the benefits to them, you will succeed at establishing a steady stream of referrals.

DATA BASE MAILINGS

The next internal marketing tactic that we will discuss is mailings from in-house data bases. The fact is that you will have names and contact information of potential customers who connected with you. Some people have asked for information about your studio or classes; others have participated in one or two classes but never became consistent users. Still others were active students at one time and no longer participate.

Regardless of how you came about these individuals names and contact information, marketing tells us that any individual who has had contact with your business is over 300% more likely to buy from you in the future than an individual who knows nothing about you or your products and services. That's powerful yes sending out mailings is one of the most underutilized marketing efforts for small businesses. Perhaps the reason is simply one of organization—i.e. taking the time to put the letter (or email) together, printing it and then mailing it. But the time and effort it takes to send out such materials is small in comparison to the potential upside.

Imagine that you have information on 100 people who know about your studio or classes but are not currently paying students. Let's further assume that you want to send out letters the "old fashioned way" in an attempt to get a better response rate. At the time of this printing, the cost of a first class stamp in the US is currently .46 cents. Let's make the math easy and round up the piece of paper and envelope to a total of .50 cents (might be a few cents more but let's keep it simple here). If you took the time to hand address the envelopes to ensure the letters got opened it is highly conceivable that you would get at least a 3% response rate. This means that you could motivate 3 individuals to come in and at least take one class. Okay, so that might not seem like much but those three—single class responses—at $15 per class would almost get you back to an even cash flow not including the time it took you to put the mailing together.

But chances are that you will get not only a 3% response rate but that at least one of those three would stay for many more than just one class! The bottom line is that taking the time to send out what are called targeted mailings to individuals who have had some kind of contact with your business will pay off in the long run. Sure, the immediate response rate might not seem great but you also have to take into consideration the value of "good will" that is generated when people get a personal letter from you inviting you to come back to class.

> " *The key with any data base mailing is to try and make it as personal as possible.*

The key with any data base mailing is to try and make it as personal as possible. Therefore, separate the data bases accordingly so you can customize different letters for specific types of prospects. The most obvious categories would be things like, called in but never showed, took one or two classes but that was it, or was a student for a period of time then dropped off. The goal is being able to draft the letter so it speaks directly to their situation.

Next, make sure you utilize technology to do simple things like merging first names on the letter. A "Dear Previous Visitor" opening certainly won't create a warm and fuzzy feeling to the recipient! Microsoft word and can easily merge a person's name from a list. (Find out more here: http://www.ehow.com/how_8230436_ merge-data-source-word-document.html.) Next, personally sign the letters and, if possible add a small note in the margin. Even something as simple as "We miss you in class" will feel very personal to the student who has been absent from the studio for some time.

[NOTE: We will be discussing e-mail marketing in a later chapter. We want to emphasize here that in a world of e-mail and text overload, a good old fashioned letter can be a highly effective form of marketing.]

Finally, as we mentioned earlier, make sure you hand address the letters. Yes, this takes time but it will ensure that the piece of mail gets opened! If you have bad penmanship (or simply don't want to do it) hire your teenage daughter or niece to do it for you. Eventually, when your business is growing and making lots of money you will look back and say, "Remember the days we used to do this at the kitchen table!"

One final thought on data base mailings is that anytime you follow up a letter with a phone call you will dramatically increase the response rate. Jay Abraham, long time direct marketing guru, has stated that response rates will jump to 7% with follow up calls. Follow up calls might not be something you are comfortable with nor have the time for and that is okay. We would be remiss, however, if we didn't at least inform you of this strategy and suggest that you consider using it if you want to maximize your direct mail effectiveness.

IN-HOUSE PROMOTIONS

One final type of internal marketing effort to mention is in-house promotions. This refers to any type of special that you might be promoting within the studio or during your class times. For example, let's say that you had hot yoga mat towels made with your studio logo on them. You had to order a high quantity to have this done but they haven't been selling too well. In an effort to get some cash flow back on these items you might offer a promotion or discount on them by putting up signs in the studio or even something as simple as making an announcement during class.

> "...running promotions to move stock is always something you should consider.

Because the mark-up on most retail is 100%, running promotions to move stock is always something you should consider. The reason being is that people love sales or specials—especially women, who comprise the majority of yoga students. Consider the significance of these very simple numbers. Let's suppose you normally retail $500 worth of drinks and yoga products a month at your studio. Sticking with a profit margin of 100% that means you profit $250 per month. Nothing to retire on but that adds up to $3,000 of income per year. Now let's suppose that by featuring one new promotional product per month you can double your monthly sales. Even assuming the margin is half the norm that would mean an additional $1,500 of profit a year. These are incredibly conservative numbers but let's re-emphasize an important point. Incremental increases in profits across multiple areas of your business will result in exponential results!

GUERRILLA MARKETING

Our focus now turns to the third pillar in the Parthenon, guerrilla marketing. Guerrilla marketing is a term used to refer to any type of marketing effort that is low cost and grass roots—i.e. done through personal relationships within your community. Don't confuse low cost with low response; guerrilla marketing may well become one of your most effective ways of attracting new customers outside of referrals. So, exactly what is guerrilla marketing? The term was coined (and trademarked) by Jay Conrad Levinson (no relation to the co-author of this book) and refers to unconventional, local efforts that a business owner can execute themselves.

With a little creativity and effort there is no limit to the number and types of guerrilla marketing efforts you can use to promote your yoga studio or class. Levinson has an entire series of books on guerrilla marketing and we highly suggest that you purchase one or two of them to reference and obtain new ideas. Below are some of the most effective guerrilla marketing ideas that the yoga studios we have worked with have used successfully.

BUSINESS CARDS

It sounds so simple that you wouldn't think it needs to be written down but we are amazed at the number of business owners who do not have professionally printed cards (or do not carry them at all times). In today's world of digital printing and the VistaPrint and GotPrint companies of the world, there is absolutely no excuse for not having full color, beautiful business cards. We will go as far as saying that if you own a studio, you should have business cards made for each of your instructors since you can have as few as 250 made at any one time for a very small cost. Doing this a) ensures that you have consistency in the look and quality of the cards your employees are passing out; and b) provides you with an opportunity to train employees on how to network with their cards, thereby helping to promote the studio.

> " *It sounds so simple that you wouldn't think it needs to be written down...*

One way to turn your business card into a much stronger lead generation tool is to have some sort of class offer or coupon printed on the back. This could be a "Free Admission to Your 1st Class" or a small discount on a first class. Of course, you would want to have all the appropriate disclaimer language at the bottom to ensure that individuals can only use such a discount once.

Another old fashioned but very effective guerrilla marketing idea is flyers. This is simply a standard 8 ½ x 11 sheet of paper, preferably color, with some sort of promotion or offer printed on it. These can then be passed out at local businesses, high traffic locations and special events in your town. If space is a restriction then it is simple to have flyers printed 2-up, meaning the flyer is actually ½ the size but with the same information.

Another effective way to use flyers is by asking students to put them at their workplace or other businesses where they have a good enough relationship whereby the owner/operator allows them to be left for their customers. Some students will be more than happy to do this, while others might need some incentive. It is simple enough to put some kind of letter or number code at the bottom of a flyer that allows you to identify the student who was responsible for the new customer.

Another twist on flyers is what is called "Tear-Off Sheets." You may recall sitting in a coffee shop and a bulletin board on the wall has a notice "Looking for a roommate." At the bottom of the paper the person put their name and phone number perpendicular to the sheet of paper and cut slits in the paper along the bottom. This allows the person who wants to contact them to simply tear off a piece with the contact information while leaving the flyer intact for the next viewer. Tear off sheets are ideal for any public bulletin board where space is limited or you don't want to leave expensive brochures or cards for fear that they will be thrown out. In addition to coffee shops many universities, trade schools, grocery stores, and community centers have these free posting boards where you could place your information. These are so low cost that if you get one paying student a year it would probably pay for itself.

Some geographical areas have businesses or organizations that specialize in distributing flyers for you. They know all the high traffic locations and can save you a lot of time and energy. Our experience has seen positive results with this type of flyering. If this type of service is not available in your area you can also hire someone to do the job. We recommend you distribute to as many places as possible. The more flyers you have up, the more potential students have a chance of seeing your message and responding to it.

Finally, it is imperative that you have flyers (and all your marketing materials) professionally designed and printed either through an online source like VistaPrint or your local print shop. You may have a small studio or yoga practice but you don't want to look small and unprofessional. Nothing screams "struggling businessperson" like a homemade marketing piece. Utilize sources like www.Fiverr.com, www.eLance.com and wwwOdesk.com to find low fee designers who will make sure your pieces look top notch and convey the image you want and need to be successful.

MUD SIGNS

If you have ever been driving around your town and see a small foam board sign attached to a wire frame that is pushed into a lawn or at the side of the road then you are familiar with mud signs. We don't know where the name came from but we know that mud signs can be highly effective. Many towns now have ordinances that make mud signs illegal. Some businesses know this, use them anyway and then get fined by the town. For them the return on investment may be worth it but for yoga studios you will want to check out your town rules before investing in the signs. Of course, mud signs can be placed on a property owner's lawn with only their permission.

Mud signs are not that expensive. One standard mud sign might cost you $39 but if you have one or two dozen made the cost can be cut in half. It will depend upon your local print shop or online source.

> **We find that mud signs are very effective when you first open your studio.**

We find that mud signs are very effective when you first open your studio. This is especially true if you can place them in high traffic areas where lots of eyeballs will see the sign. Of course, using the right language is important because you have very limited space to convey your message. Remember the more words on a mud sign the smaller the print! So, keeping it short but enticing is always best. For example:

New Yoga Studio
Free first class.
Call 800-555-7009.

One word of caution about mud signs to those of you who are in a highly competitive market. If you have multiple yoga studios in your area, do not be surprised if your mud signs go missing. Not unlike elections, it is common for competitors to steal your signs and pitch them in the nearest dumpster, thereby preventing prospects from seeing your offer. May sound terrible but it can happen. An alternative to mud signs is sandwich board signs that can also be made at your local print shop. The advantage to these is that you can easily put them right out front of your studio and they can sit on any surface. They are extremely portable so you can take them in at the end of the day. These types of signs are particularly effective in high traffic locations.

DOOR HANGARS

Before you dismiss this idea know that door hangars aren't just for doors anymore! Door hangars are one of the most versatile guerrilla marketing materials you can utilize because their format allows for use in a variety of places. First, let's make sure you understand what a door hangar is; it is a rectangular, card stock piece—approximately 4" x 11" that has a circle cut out of the top and a slit on the side of the circle that allows someone to easily hang the piece on a door knob, hence the name door hangar. Guerrilla marketers have found out that these good looking, double sided marketing pieces also easily hang over coat hangers at clothing stores, dry cleaners and uniform shops as well as rear view mirrors at car dealerships and local car washes.

Now you may be asking, "But why would one of those businesses want to put my yoga marketing material in front of their customers?" Maybe the owner is one of your students and yoga has changed their life or perhaps one of your instructors or students just happens to know the owner or manager. There may even be a situation where, if you own a studio, there is an opportunity to do some joint marketing. For example, how about having the local sports shop put your door hangar on all the yoga clothing they sell and, in return, you give their promotional material into the hands of your students! It would be a win/win for both businesses and at virtually no cost. Are you beginning to think of other possibilities? We hope so.

Literally we could do an entire chapter on guerrilla marketing ideas but because there are dozens of books on the subject there isn't a need for that here. Our goal was to expose you to a few proven concepts and then allow your own creativity to brainstorm some good ideas. Creativity combined with knowledge and understanding of your community and student body is a winning combination. We'd like to close this section by offering you some tips on how to maximize your guerrilla marketing efforts.

- Leverage the relationships you have with friends, family members and long-time students to identify guerrilla marketing opportunities.

- When possible print full color materials so they pop and look professional.

- Track your print quantities, numbers distributed and how many pieces were left over at the end of each promotion. Use this information to make better printing decisions in the future.

- Remember to put an offer and expiration date on all your promotional materials. It is human nature to procrastinate and expiration dates help to move people into action sooner rather than later.

COMMUNITY MARKETING

Community marketing, sometimes referred to as community outreach, refers to anything you do that builds good will in the community. Although these efforts are still part of your marketing Parthenon, they are not intended to immediately drive new students to your studio or class. Rather, the goal is to show that you're an active participant in the community, helping to create a feeling of trust and encouraging locals to "want" to do business with you.

> *There are many ways in which you can engage in community marketing.*

There are many ways in which you can engage in community marketing. Donating your time to local charity events and causes is one way to get involved without having to actually organize something yourself. And it is good karma! You could put together a team of students to participate in a local walking event that is raising money for a good cause. At the holiday you could collect donations for things like Toys for Tots, the local food bank or a coat drive. And perhaps the most overlooked, yet powerful way to gain community exposure is sending out press releases on happenings and news from your studio. Because press release services report to all the internet search engines, they can be a particularly powerful way to create brand awareness and loyalty. Best of all there are press release services that are absolutely free! A simple and free way to get your press release out is through a service called PR Log (www.PRLog.net). Since it's totally free, there's no reason why every business isn't sending out regular press releases. You'll also want to make a list of your local newspaper, radio and television media and send them your press releases as well.

Many small businesses are overwhelmed with the basic marketing functions and day to day operation of their business. As a result most do not spend a lot of time on community marketing. If you can get organized and do just a few things annually with this pillar it will strengthen your exposure and your business image.

PUTTING IT ALL TOGETHER

We have outlined for you some primary marketing tactics in four of the six Parthenon pillars. This is a good place to stop and revisit the strategy behind the Parthenon approach. Remember you do NOT want to rely on one or two marketing practices. You want to build stability in your marketing plan by having new customers coming from a variety of sources each and every month. This means you want to be doing multiple marketing tactics within each of the primary pillars every single month. Just like sales, marketing is a numbers game; the more efforts you participate in the more successful you will be.

Now that you understand the strategy and the tactics, take some time to start putting together your marketing plan so you can ensure maximum success of your studio or practice.

CHAPTER 5
INTERNET MARKETING

We live in a digital society. The majority of people have a smart phone or iPad within reach at all times. When we want to find something we no longer ask or look it up with something as archaic as a phone book; we simply Google it! And, since all devices that use the internet are attached to an IP (internet provider) address, when we search for a business, locally optimized businesses will show up first.

Customers searching on the web will immediately go to a business' web page to make an initial screening; they will check reviews on the most popular sites and many will go to the Better Business Bureau on-line. All of these things are done in an attempt to make an educated decision as to whether or not your business is a) going to meet their needs and wants, and b) is reputable.

> *...you MUST have a solid internet presence in order to succeed...*

What all of this means is that you MUST have a solid internet presence in order to succeed in the today's competitive business environment. The challenge for small business owners is managing the multitude of internet tools. A website, Facebook, Twitter, YouTube, Pinterest, a Blog and potentially a half dozen other options make it overwhelming for many—especially for those over the age of 40 who did not grow up using these tools! There are entire books that focus on each one of these subjects so our goal is to provide you with a solid understanding of the key things you need to be doing to have a strong internet presence.

INTERNET VS. SOCIAL MEDIA

For the purposes of this book we want to start by defining two distinct aspects of marketing that involve using the World Wide Web. They often get referred to and put in the same "marketing bucket" but we believe they are distinctly different, hence need separation. The two areas are "internet marketing" and "social media marketing."

Internet marketing refers to anything you do on the internet that involves your website, opt-in pages, on-line advertising, and the use of an auto responder system (we will explain this in a later chapter). Social media marketing refers to anything you do that involves the use of ANY social media platform. This would include, but is not limited to, the more popular sites like Facebook, Twitter, YouTube, and Pinterest.

What is the primary difference between internet marketing and social media marketing and why are we even making the distinction? First, we make the distinction because it helps the business owner/operator to break down this huge marketing space into two distinct areas. Ultimately this makes creating a plan easier. Second, the difference is slight but important because it helps to identify more potentially qualified customers. Let's further explain this second distinction.

Imagine there is a woman Jane who lives in your town and is within the age and income demographics of your customer profile. She had done yoga years ago when she lived in another state but fell out of the habit. It's now New Year's and she is considering going back to yoga. It is safe to say that she is a qualified prospect that could become a future student. This person will most likely go to the internet and do a Google search for yoga classes in her area. If you have done things right your company or name will come up on the Google Local Listings and she will click through to your website. Furthermore you may have bought some Google AdWords and she clicks through that way.

Now imagine a second woman named Susan, who also lives in your town and is within the age and income demographics of your customer profile. Susan, however, has never done yoga. Of course, she knows of it but for whatever reason she had never considered it. Susan has a friend named Michelle who starts going to yoga at your studio and makes a post on her Facebook timeline about the wonderful yoga class she is taking and how she has lost some weight and is getting in great shape participating. Furthermore Michelle "Likes" your Facebook Page. Because Susan is Facebook friends with Michelle she sees her post that she has "Liked" your studio. Because of these posts Susan clicks through to your Facebook Page and ultimately comes to your website to learn more about your studio or classes.

What these two scenarios exemplify is a primary difference between internet marketing and social media marketing. Internet marketing is often reaching people who are looking for your product or services where social media marketing can be very influential in creating new prospects. Although this is a generalization it is an important distinction for getting the most out of all your World Wide Web efforts.

> " *...social media marketing can be very influential in creating new prospects.*

This chapter is going to focus on internet marketing. We will discuss how to get the most from your website, introduce you to the concept of capture mechanisms, and wrap things up by exploring online advertising.

YOUR WEBSITE

Regardless of whether you own a studio or are just growing your own class practice, you need to have a website. It will become the hub of all your marketing activity. Not having a website would be equivalent to not being listed in the phone book 20 years ago—simply unacceptable. A large percentage of people looking for products or services start their search online. If you don't have an online presence then you are missing a lot of opportunity to connect with potential students. Just as importantly, you are failing to provide current students a way to connect with when away from classes.

The first step in setting up a web site is getting a URL (Web address). Many instructors who don't own a studio often question, "If I don't own a studio then what should I get for a website address?" Certainly one simple answer would be to use your personal name. If that isn't available because you have a common name then you could add the word "Yoga" to the end of your name. For example, www.SusanSmithYoga.com.

If you haven't opened a yoga studio yet we highly suggest trying to find a name where the URL is available. There are many reasons why you ideally want to secure the URL for your business' name.

For one, it is easier for branding. Let's suppose you call your studio Waterfront Yoga but find out that someone else has already taken the URL and there are 6 other yoga studios around the world that have the same name. If a prospect drives by your studio and sees your sign, comes home and Google's "Waterfront

Yoga" they may not actually find you on the first page of search listings. This is particularly plausible in the early days of your business if you haven't done the necessary work with search engine optimization.

Second, it will be much easier for all your marketing if the URL and your business name matches. Using the same example above you might have secured the state corporate name "Waterfront Yoga" but could only get www.WaterfrontYogaRI.com. Doesn't seem like the end of the world (and it's not) but it certainly makes it easier on things like T-shirts and brochures when the two match.

Finally, it is better for search engine optimization if the business name and the URL match. Again, it won't make or break your business but having the two match will result in faster optimization. This is true for things that you will post on the internet as well as when customers refer to your business. Think about the example we have been using. If a student goes to write something on their Facebook status about the great class they just took, they will probably reference the company name—Waterfront Yoga—not the URL.

> "...seek out a professional designer to help you with building your web site.

Of course, once you have your website it will be important to choose a format that is easy to set up and maintain from a business perspective as well as easy to navigate from a visitor's perspective. We suggest that you get your website done using Wordpress. It is common, user-friendly for everyone and has lots of plug-ins and other applications that allow you to add schedules, link to PayPal and even integrate bookings programs. We highly recommend that you seek out a professional designer to help you with building your web site. This will save you a lot of headaches. Let's turn our discussion now to some important marketing elements.

UNDERSTANDING WEBSITE GOALS

When it comes to marketing, it is important to keep a perspective on the specific goals each marketing effort should be accomplishing. This is particularly true with a website. Too many businesses complicate their website and make it cumbersome for the customer to navigate. Your goal is to keep it simple.

There are four specific outcomes that your website must accomplish.

1. Establish a level of credibility in the eyes of the consumer by looking professional, up to date, and being user-friendly.

2. Provide existing customers with information they need and want. This would include things like schedules, instructor profiles, pricing, and on-line bookings (if your studio does that).

3. Provide prospects with enough information about your studio and/or classes so they can make an educated decision whether or not to try your services.

4. Be a lead generator.

Although each of these functions is important and necessary to a successful website, it is the fourth function—lead generation—that most business operators fail to accomplish. Ironically enough, lead generation and building a database will have the greatest long-term impact on whether or not your business is marginally successful or wildly successful. We know that is a bold statement but we believe that by the time you are finished with this chapter you will understand and agree with it. So, let's step back and discuss your website goals.

YOUR PRIMARY GOAL!

When ANYONE who is <u>not</u> currently a student visits your website the primary goal is to incent them to give you their name and e-mail address. This allows you to build an internal database of interested prospects with whom you can directly communicate. This is a HUGE distinction that you must understand.

You do NOT want to wait for an interested prospect to finally push through procrastination and come take a class with you 3, 6 or 12 months after their initial viewing of your website! Rather, you want interested students to identify themselves so you can motivate them sooner rather than later to come try a yoga class at your studio.

Certainly your website must be attractive, provide your existing students with all the proper scheduling info, and give visitors enough information so they want to check out your studio or classes. However, a website by itself is NOT a pro-active marketing tool. The only way that you turn a static website into a generator of possible future customers is to add elements that help you build a list.

ENTER THE CAPTURE MECHANISM

Capture mechanism is a generic term for any tool that entices prospects to give you their names and email addresses. You have probably seen many web pages with capture mechanisms before. You may have even entered your name and email address for something "free." Here are some examples of some capture mechanisms.

ENTICING ALL VISITORS

When deciding upon what capture mechanisms will work best, it is important to recognize that there will be two distinctly different types of prospect-visitors to your website. First you will have the visitor that is looking for a yoga studio or class and wants information that will help him or her make a decision about visiting. Second you will have visitors who are thinking about trying out yoga but have absolutely no experience. This visitor might want a lot more information before they will feel comfortable visiting the studio or trying a class. That may seem like an obvious statement but recognizing those two different prospects identifies an important marketing strategy.

You MUST have at least two different capture mechanisms that will appeal to both types of visitors to your website.

> Remember that your goal is to entice all visitors to give you their name and e-mail address.

Remember that your goal is to entice all visitors to give you their name and e-mail address. Therefore, for the person who is ready to come try your classes you will want to have some kind of trial or discount coupon. For the person who thinks they might be interested in yoga you ideally would have some kind of free informational booklet or educational video. These types of materials will give them a better understanding about why they should try out yoga, and ideally gives information that makes them feel more confident about trying yoga. In either instance, the visitor will need to give their name and e-mail in order to have access to the coupon or information.

THE IRRESISTIBILITY OF "FREE"

When working with studio owners we often hear objections about giving away free enticements. With free booklets or videos their fear is that too many people outside their geographic area will download the information and clutter up their data base. And when it comes to giving out a discounted or free class pass the universal concern is that there will be abuse. These may both be valid concerns, but neither one is a problem.

First of all, with online data bases and auto responder programs it really doesn't matter if you have people outside your geographic area opting in because technology does all the work. You never know when someone from out of the area will be visiting your town or knows people from the area. And you never know; perhaps you will be offering a retreat in some interesting destination. In this instance people from out of your area who practice yoga could be viable participants. But this will only happen if you stay in touch with them regularly with your database efforts.

Second, although the possibility of abuse always exists when you put some kind of free or discount class coupon on your website, that isn't a marketing problem; that is an operational problem! The goal of marketing is to get potential students through your doors. If there is an occasional abuser then let Karma catch up with them. For you, capture mechanisms that offer free stuff WILL result in more visitors to your classes. End of subject.

Of course, "free" is nothing new or revolutionary in the world of marketing. Whether it's a free taste of a new product featured at the grocery store, or the no-risk 30-day in-home trial of an expensive Tempurpedic mattress, good marketers know that if consumers can experience (and enjoy) a product or service first-hand, they'll be much more likely to buy. Bottom line is that free is irresistible to many consumers and that works in your favor as a business using capture mechanism strategies.

Because having capture mechanisms is so important to your website's success, let's take some time to outline the key components needed to maximize their success.

CLASS PASS OR DISCOUNT COUPON

- The first thing you need to decide is whether or not you will have a completely free class pass or a discounted coupon on your website. Obviously, the free pass will result in more opt-ins than the discount coupon but this is a decision that you will need to make based on many factors. Is your studio or class brand new and you therefore have many spaces to fill? If you have other instructors working for you, have you outlined the rules with them so they understand that first time visitors will be free or discounted? If you have a studio, do you have the operational and administrative functions in place to minimize coupon abuse?

Only you can make the ultimate decision as to whether or not to offer a "Free First Class" coupon or just a discounted class fee. The important thing is that you use one or the other. DO NOT have a statement on your website that says, "Drop in and your first class is free." NO! Remember the goal is to capture the name and e-mail address so you can properly follow up. Believe it or not, many people will opt-in for a pass or coupon and never show up unless you have future communication with them. This is simply human nature. Having the opt-in puts you in control, not sitting around waiting for an interested prospect to visit.

- Second, make sure that you do not require too much information in the capture mechanism. Very often a business will offer a free coupon or discount certificate to the visitor but they require them to practically give their life's information in order to get the offer. This is a HUGE mistake. In marketing we refer to this as "lowering or raising the barrier to entry." Simply stated, if you make it easy for the customer to get the item being offered then you will get a higher response rate. Make it more difficult and you create a "barrier to entry" and you will get fewer takers. We suggest that at this stage in your relationship with a potential student that you only require name and e-mail address. NOT first name and last name. Just "Name." And, do not require a phone number! Many business operators have the attitude that "If they want the free pass or discount coupon then they have to give me their phone number." This is the wrong attitude and will result in many, many less opt-ins because most customers don't want the business to call them! You need to be happy and content with the name and e-mail knowing you can now at least follow up with them. To the right is a simple example of what the opt-in box for in capture mechanism might look like.

- Third, make sure that all your capture mechanisms are connected to an autoresponder system that automatically delivers the pass, coupon or informational link directly to the person's e-mail. In the next chapter we will discuss autoresponders and how to select one that is right for you. Suffice it to say here that all your capture mechanisms must utilize technology to maximize new customers and minimize administrative work in the follow up process.

- Fourth, to help minimize abuse, make sure that the downloadable coupon has language on it stating, "First time visitors and local residents only."

ONLINE ADVERTISING

You've probably have heard many stories about people or firms that used online advertising and made themselves loads of money. It does happen! I personally know many people who have succeeded with a variety of online advertising strategies. Sadly, there are many more individuals who started out with big hopes, but, lacking the proper education or any plan spent a ton of money on advertising, with no results. If you are considering using online advertising then here is some essential information you need to know.

One of the most common forms of online advertising is pay-per-click, often referred to as "PPC." As the name implies, every time a viewer clicks onto the advertisement displayed on their screen the advertiser pays a certain amount. The amount you pay is determined either by negotiating with the specific website that will display your ad or, in the case of sites like Google, Yahoo and MSN, by "bidding." You actually bid against other businesses and individuals for your ad to be displayed when the user types in certain keywords or phrases. Costs can range from pennies-per-click to many dollars-per-click, all depending upon the marketplace's supply and demand.

As you can imagine, today's online advertising has many levels of complexity. In addition to a deep understanding of keywords and searches, you must know how to formulate an effective online ad (which is very different than traditional ads) and how to establish filters so that you get qualified clicks, resulting in qualified leads. At the risk of being redundant, the biggest mistake most businesses make is expecting clicks to immediately turn into sales. That may be the case for some products and services, but not typically for yoga studios because you aren't selling a product that someone buys on the internet. Rather, the person is coming to your site to gather information and, if interested, will probably come to your studio to take a single class. This is NOT to say that some kind of PPC isn't effective; we personally know studios that use Google AdWords very effectively. However, it is important to recognize that IF the campaign is going to be effective certain things must be done correctly.

We'd really need to write a separate book to do justice to the subject of online advertising. Before you venture into this area, we recommend that you invest in the book *Adwords for*

Dummies. Once you have that publication, consider the following "checklist" as an additional resource that applies specifically to yoga studios.

- Always have your PPC ad re-direct to an opt-in page, NOT the home page of your website. Unless you have a good reason not to give the first class for free or some kind of discount coupon, this should be at least one of the offers on this opt-in page. Remember that your goal is to capture their name and e-mail address so you can follow up.

- Make sure your opt-in page is professionally done, attractive and compelling. Give the visitor enough information to get engaged and think, "This is a place that I would like to visit."

- Be target specific! You are a small, local business and don't want clicks from someone outside of your market area. (Remember, you pay PER click.) This can be done using a variety of tools as well as specific language. For example, include your town name in the headline of your advertisement minimizing clicks outside of local area residents.

- Test, test and then test. The beauty of PPC is that you get immediate data on your click and conversion rate. In the early days you want to test the major components of the ad to maximize success. These include, but are not limited to, the headline, offer and the opt-on mechanics. Be sure to test one element at a time and continue to test and tweak until you are getting the best click and conversion rate possible.

FACEBOOK ADS

We don't want to totally scare you off from using pay-per-click advertising. Like the other major players, Facebook offers a pay-per-click option that differs in its ability to very narrowly target where your ad is displayed based on user profile information. To start with, each individual's Facebook profile has basics like age, gender and physical location, but can also include such information as marital status, education level, and occupation. Facebook lets you find very precise audiences by using both demographics and psychographic filters. You can stipulate that only 40-year-old women married within a 5-mile radius of your business will view your ad! Even more amazing is the ability to target keywords within someone's profile—things like television shows, movies, books, sports, and yes, even the words yoga and variations of this keyword. You can add "Oprah" or the movie "Eat, Pray, Love" to your filter, ensuring that only those people who matched *every* chosen criteria would see your ad. The result is that you can create a very localized and highly targeted audience, but not high volume. Best of all, there's very little financial risk: You can specify exactly how much money you want to spend each day and how many days you want to run the campaign. Finally, by using the right marketing strategy you can build a list and track your conversion rates.

> *Even more amazing is the ability to target keywords within someone's profile...*

Certainly we encourage you to further educate yourself on the best way to use Facebook ads. There are many books and online resources you can invest in. However, Facebook offers quite a bit of information on the subject that will at least get you started. You can find that information at https://www.facebook.com/business/ads.

FOCUS ON THE LIST

Before we end this chapter it is important to step back and get clear on the primary objective of all your internet activities. Your goal is to use various internet tools to drive prospects into your data base. This accomplishes two very important things in marketing. First, it creates your own list of more qualified prospects. Second, when you manage the list you are in control of communicating with those prospects.

Companies pay top dollar to buy quality prospect lists. The more qualified the list the more it will cost a business to buy that list. When you build your own list you are saving lots of money. For one you don't have to buy the list. Secondly your conversion ratio of those prospects becoming members will be higher than a purchased list. This makes your customer acquisition cost lower because of a greater response rate.

What all this means is that you must be able to build your online database. Unfortunately there is a lot of confusion about which database program to use and many small business operators who are new to internet marketing really don't know which features are important and which aren't. So, let's move on to the next chapter where we will de-mystify the world of contact management and provide you with an understanding and checklist of exactly what you need and why.

CHAPTER 6

THE IMPORTANCE OF THE RIGHT CONTACT MANAGEMENT SYSTEM

A contact management system (CMS) is nothing more than a software program that stores information about your prospects and customers and allows you to communicate with them. Years ago a business would buy such a program and load it onto their computers. This meant they needed to buy upgrades every time a new version was released. Today's top contact management programs are all hosted online and updates happen automatically without you having to do anything. Aside from the obvious benefits of not needing to pay or hassle with upgrades, another benefit of being online is that your data is being stored "in the cloud" and accessible to you from any computer, anywhere you can access the internet.

There are many, many contact management programs available. Some are well known and have been around for years while many are smaller providers who are trying to win over a share of the market. At the end of this chapter we will give you our recommendations but it is first necessary to understand the various features that you will want in any program you choose.

EMAIL SUBMISSIONS

It may sound obvious but the first thing your contact management program must have is the ability to accept opt-in e-mail submissions when a prospect requests something you have offered online. For example, when a visitor wants to download the class pass on your website you want the information they submit (name and e-mail) to automatically go into the contact management system.

> "...but the first thing your contact management program must have is the ability to accept opt-in e-mail...

This is pretty standard but in the "old days" of the internet a person would submit information that was sent to the owner's e-mail in-box and then that information would need to be manually entered into a database. This had several flaws. One is that the process was subject to human error—i.e. entering the information incorrectly into the database. Another problem is that in today's over-e-mailed world, SPAM filters can recognize the IP address of the e-mail sender. If the person who is getting the e-mail didn't put their name into the database, thereby requesting the information, future communications will often being identified as SPAM and never be delivered to the person.

By directly accepting the person's information there is less work for you, the business operator, and there is better communication between you and the person requesting the information.

EASY CUSTOM OPT-IN FORM GENERATOR

The next item on your contact management system (CMS) wish list is ease of creating opt-in forms. Many of you could be designing your own website and certainly most of you will initially undertake the management of your website, which will include your CMS. Having the system automatically accept the e-mail submissions is one thing, but ensuring that the system is easy to use is very different. Some can be incredibly complex and that usually results in frustration. Therefore, find out if the program has a wizard or at minimum, an installation guide that walks you through the process step by step. Also, does the program allow you to customize the opt-in boxes/ fields or are you required to use only standard options. This might eventually be a painful limitation.

EASE OF INTEGRATING INTO YOUR PRESENT WEBSITE

Sometimes a program makes customizing opt-in forms easy, but it's a nightmare to integrate them into your webpage. Some forms may not work well with whatever design language created the web page. And the opt-in box is useless if you can't integrate it into your web page. If you are unfamiliar with any product, find other people who are using it and ask them how easily they can integrate opt-in forms onto their web pages.

ABILITY TO SEGMENT LISTS AT THE OPT-IN POINT

Though all the features we are discussing are equally important to overall functionality, this one—being able to segment lists at the point of opt-in—is critical. Suppose you have discount class passes for first time visitors and you are using that offer in a variety of marketing mediums; on your website, on your business card and on a guerrilla marketing flyer. You will want a system that puts each individual opt-in into a folder that identifies exactly where they received the pass. A contact management system that "dumps" every opt-in into one central database won't give you this option.

> *...being able to segment lists at the point of opt-in — is critical.*

Therefore, you want a system to let you create opt-in boxes for each capture mechanism source (even if it is the same offer), so that names go into a database "folder" unique for each source. If not designed specifically for internet marketing, contact management systems seldom offer this feature. This is a major limitation because it doesn't allow you to create follow up sequences to specific groups of prospects. Once you begin building your lists, you'll greatly appreciate this necessary process and the feature that lets you accomplish it. So, even if you don't completely understand this feature know that it is very important.

NUMBER OF AUTORESPONDER SEQUENCES ALLOWED

In internet marketing, an opt-in box connected to a unique database used to send back emails or information to prospective customers is called an "autoresponder." The contact management system's primary function is to automatically send pre-written emails to any prospect that opts-in. This ensures that the proper follow-ups get sent without some human having to physically do it.

In our earlier example of using a class pass as a capture mechanism, we cited three places it would be promoted—on a website, on a business card, and a guerrilla marketing flyer. So your contact management system would have three different databases, or segmented lists. Therefore, you want any system to allow an unlimited number of autoresponders and segmented lists.

Every software program uses its own lingo. One may term your segmented lists "campaigns," another may call them "email lists." Once you begin working with opt-in pages and data base collection, all this will become clear. For now, to ensure that we are speaking the same language, let's refer to a group of prospects within your database as a "sub-list."

You may find it hard to believe at this point, but you could eventually have hundreds of sub-lists. Therefore, it is very important that you choose a database program that is going to allow you to track all your marketing efforts in a very targeted, almost scientific way. Below is a list of features we believe are important in your selection of a program.

ALLOWABLE FOLLOW-UPS PER AUTORESPONDER

Once you're sure a system allows for an unlimited number of segmented lists, the next important feature you want is the ability to send an unlimited number of so-called "autoresponder" messages to prospects in those lists.

Autoresponder messages are exactly that; they automatically send pre-programmed messages to the names in a specific sub-list, *and* in a specific pre-determined sequence. Admittedly, trying to write an example of how this works is much more difficult than if someone physically showed you. Therefore, in addition to the written explanation below here is a link to a short video that visually walks you through understanding this: www.letsdoyoga.com/yogabusiness.

Let's review our earlier marketing example. You were offering a class-pass in three different locations: on your website, on your business card and on a guerrilla marketing flyer. You want people who opt-in to receive 1) receive the pass they asked for, and 2) receive three reminder messages thereafter. However, since you want to track the opt-ins from each separate marketing effort you will need to create three different sub-lists in your contact management software. "Class Pass on Website," "Class Pass on business card," and "Class Pass on supermarket flyer" (as you may have many different flyer locations you want to track).

Within each individual sub-list, you will prepare a series of follow-up messages that the system will send automatically. Each message is identified by subject matter and time sequence—that is, when the message will be sent to given people, depending on the day they opted-in. Continuing with our example, if you clicked on the sub-list "Class pass on business card, you would see the following table:

Message #	Days Delay	Subject
1	0	"Here's your class pass!"
2	4	"How was your class?"
3	10	"Tips on getting the most of your class"

In this example, the first of the three messages would go out immediately when a person submits information on the squeeze page's opt-in form—hence the "zero" days delay. The second message would go out four days later, and the third 10 days after the opt-in date. Each of your sub lists can use the exact same messages or they can be slightly modified to make them more personal to that specific marketing location.

> " You want the ability to program an unlimited number of messages into your system.

Two important points you need to understand:

1. You want the ability to program an unlimited number of messages into your system. An individual may opt in for a pass or some information but take months to finally make it to your class or studio. You want to continue a relationship with that person so when they are ready to finally participate you are on the top of their mind. To the traditional marketer this seems bizarre, but a system with no limits on follow-up messages is what makes internet marketing so powerful!

2. No matter when people opt-in to your squeeze page, they'll receive messages in the exact "delay-sequence" established in the autoresponder. Therefore, in our example above, if you opted in on June 1st, you'd receive message #1 (the class pass) immediately. You'd get message #2, four days later on June 5th, then message #3 six days after that, on June 11th. Obviously, if I first opt in on May 10th, I'd get message #1 that same day; message #2 on the 15th, and message #3 on the 21st.

Each message will be sent in the exact same pre-set sequence, 365 days of the year. Because of this you will never put any time-sensitive details into an "automatic" autoresponder. For example, you would never create an invitation to an upcoming pranayama class **unless** that class is given regularly on a particular night, say the third Tuesday of every month. This may seem elementary, but many people put a date-specific message ("Special New Year's class with Famous Instructor") in their autoresponders and then wonder why no one is responding—because for anyone getting that automatic message after January 1st, the invitation is no longer valid!

You can change the messages if you want, but the whole beauty of the system is that after you've tweaked a message sequence to elicit the highest level of responses, you don't need to change it. The system requires virtually no human intervention!

EMAIL "BROADCAST" CAPABILITY

Although you want to "fix" your autoresponder messages and let automation do the work, there will be instances where you want to send certain prospects a time specific email or invitation. Suppose you've compiled a list of prospects that opted in for a class pass but have not come in to use it yet. Perhaps you decide to run some kind of summer special on a 10-class pass. These people are ideal targets to know about this offering. To reach them with a time specific message, use an email broadcast, where you send a single message to a specific list of people.

In our example, you would want anyone who opted-in for a class pass to learn about the summer special. Within this category, you have at least three unique lists: people who opted-in on the website, those who opted-in off one of your business cards and those who saw a flyer. Regardless of how many sub-lists in your contact management system, you want the capability to broadcast email to individual lists *or* to *send* them to several sub-lists at once. Therefore, make sure any contact management system you choose can do that.

It's also important that when emailing to multiple sub-lists, your software can eliminate duplicate addresses. For example, say you broadcast an invitation to a special yoga workshop to three or more sub-lists. Some prospects may have opted-in on more than one list and will get that many invitations unless your software checks that only one email goes out to each address.

MAIL MERGE

Broadcast email is great, but the mail merge feature gives it a touch of class, letting you personalize emails. The more you can make the e-mail feel like it is going to that one prospect, the greater your response rate will be. People automatically pay more attention to any email with their name on it compared, to one that begins, "Dear Friend . . ."

If your contact management system has no mail merge feature built in, you'll need to perform a very complex process: export names out of the database, format the file, and then enter it into an email program. The more complicated it is, the less likely you'll do it. Set yourself up for the highest success by choosing a system with a mail-merge feature. Although this is a fairly standard feature in today's programs it is something you just want to make sure you have.

TAKE A DEEP BREATH AND RELAX

At this point, some of these internet marketing features may seem overwhelming. But an easy solution is a program called Kick Start Cart. (www.OurFavoriteCart.com). Don't let the word "cart" mislead you, because this total contact management system has all the "must have" features: database, autoresponder, broadcast functions and much, much more. We personally know many people who have been using this system for many years and many of the gurus in the internet marketing industry recommend it for two primary reasons. One, it has all the necessary features and two, it is cost effective. And they're smart; they offer a free trial! During a free 3-week trial, you can access all of Our Favorite Cart's training videos and resource materials, educating yourself in the process.

Some people ask us, "Do you own this product? Is that why you recommend it?" No but we use it. Further, we have recommended it to so many people that we enrolled in their affiliate program. This means that if you end up using the system—at a cost of $34.95 per month ($59.95/month when you upgrade to the shopping cart), we get a small commission. This won't change the cost to you. The company simply wants happy users to refer their friends and associates (just like you do).

EXPLORING OTHER OPTIONS

Although we are biased about which contact management program to use, it's important that you make a final decision based on what is best for your needs. Therefore, we would be remiss if we didn't at least mention other programs available.

Often small businesses tell us that they are already using Constant Contact and have the expectation that this will work with their new internet marketing efforts. Yes, Constant Contact is really easy to use and has lots of templates to make html email formats but, at the time of this printing, it has a couple of very big limitations. One is that you are limited to 10 autoresponders and can only have 5 active at any given time. Because you are going to eventually have all your marketing efforts driven to squeeze pages you will need dozens, if not hundreds of autoresponders. Second and most importantly, you are limited to 6 follow up messages in any autoresponder sequence. Because your goal is to move prospects down the behavioral change process, you need the ability to send them messages for many months directly through your autoresponder (not email broadcasts). This is why having a system that gives you unlimited messages is critical. For us these two are deal-killers.

One other option that we can endorse is a program called AWeber. This program has ready to use templates and unlimited autoresponders and messages as well as some good analytics. The only drawback is that it doesn't have a shopping cart built into it. This means if you ever want to sell or deliver products you will have to use a payment portal like PayPal. With OurFavoriteCart you have the option to add your own credit card processing right into the system. That is a nice feature for online buyers. Some other up and coming systems that we know of but not enough to make a recommendation are MailChimp, iContact and InfusionSoft. There are many more out there if you do a search. Do your homework and try to find others successfully using those systems before making a choice. Most importantly, make sure they have some kind of free trial so you can play with it for a week or two before making a choice.

Regardless of your final decision, keep in mind two things. Changing from one contact management system to another is a nightmare. Second, no matter what contact management program you decide on there will be a learning curve. Often the people responsible for marketing efforts don't gravitate towards detailed tasks. Learning these types of software programs can cause frustration. Make sure whatever system you move forward with has a good online learning center and a help desk. You may have to pay for help after the first 30-days (typical with most) but so long as it is available you will be able to get answers and additional training.

CHAPTER 7
SOCIAL MEDIA MARKETING

With a good foundation of traditional and online marketing set, we can now turn our focus to social media marketing. Social media has become one of the fastest forms of marketing for small businesses. It is inexpensive, fast, and has the potential to reach lots of prospects. The challenge is that the category is vast and changes at a pace that makes print materials almost obsolete before they make it to the market! As a result, our goal in this chapter is to discuss the key networks you should consider using, help demystify the process of getting started and, most importantly outline the strategy you should be following with whatever social media marketing you end up using. We suggest that once you identify key social networks that you want to focus on, that you find additional resources and training to maximize your proficiency within that medium.

"Social networking" is a generic term for any activity that fosters people's interaction online. The most familiar, popular social networking sites are Facebook, Twitter, YouTube, Pinterest and, for business, LinkedIn. Online coupon sites include Groupon, Living Social and Amazon Local are also important and widely used social networks for small business. All these sites encourage people to converse openly and share information, contacts and deals—hence the term "networking."

Because there are a handful of very popular sites, many people don't realize there are hundreds of social networking groups—probably thousands if you count those among small private groups. Though you won't try to engage with more than a handful of these networks, the numbers demonstrate the mediums' popularity in the internet world—and their power. Every day, more and more people connect through social networks, sharing information, likes, dislikes and experiences—both personal and professional. Engaging in social networks lets you share and network too.

There is no guarantee that social networking will bring you lots of new students but chances are that if you use it correctly it will increase your exposure and attract new prospects.

THE SOCIAL NETWORKING PITFALL

Most yoga teachers and studio owners already have at least a Facebook page. When attending our seminars attendees often say, "I have a few hundred friends on Facebook, but I never really know whether or not I am getting new students because of it."

Anytime a business makes a comment like this regarding social networking we know that they simply aren't using the medium correctly. One question uncovers the truth. "How many of your Facebook (or other social media) posts end with some kind of link that brings the reader to an opt-in page?"

Almost always, the answer is "None" and therein lays the problem. So, before we move on to any discussion of specific social media sites, let's stop and get very clear on the ONE strategy that you MUST employ if you want your social networking efforts to result in new students:

> *with social networking you have to follow some unspoken rules about not being too sales orientated...*

119

No matter what the activity, the fundamental goal of all your market-ing efforts is to build a huge list of interested prospects! Therefore, everything you do must lead the prospect to a capture mechanism where they are enticed to give you their name and e-mail address.

This same fundamental goal holds true for social networking. Of course, with social networking you have to follow some unspoken rules about not being too sales orientated but that is easy to do once you understand how.

ETIQUETTE IN *SOCIAL* MEDIA MARKETING

Picture yourself at a neighbor's party. You see people you know and head over to join them. You are all talking about golf and getting longer drives when a stranger walks up to the group and breaks in with, "Let me tell you about this awesome driver made of titanium that my company sells. Because I'm part of your conversation, I'm offering it to you today at this special discount."

Members of your conversation would be offended because he broke an unspoken rule: You don't try to sell things at a social gathering; at least not overtly. On the other hand, suppose that same stranger quietly entered the conversation. When his turn came, he mentioned the success of his golf game, the type of driver he used, and its space-age technology. Several people started asking him questions about it and he provided answers and ended with saying, "I can send you a brochure if you want."

No pressure, no selling. If someone asked him for more information, he'd simply provide it, with no urging to buy. Sure, some in the group might be wary, suspecting that he speaks highly of the golf club because he sells them for the manufacturer. But ultimately those that choose to get more information can decide for themselves, maybe even give it a test drive.

You must follow this same approach—or "etiquette" with social media marketing.

Yes, what we are doing is marketing, but you must be careful not to go on social networks and overtly promote or advertise your business or services. This is why you will place calls to action at the bottom of your social-network posts. Adding a link that takes readers some place where they can get more *free* information is acceptable—provided that you have already given them valuable information as a lead-in. Constantly repeating a post that says, "Come try us out" or "We're open for business" is not acceptable and will ultimately frustrate those individuals on that social network.

CONTENT IS KING

One of the most important elements of a successful social media strategy is content. Consumers are looking for quality information, and so are the search engines. The more quality information you share, the more search engines will find you and the more prospects will trust you.

Unfortunately, many small businesses use social media as a real time newsletter regarding their happenings. "6am class cancelled on Tuesday," "New class added to Saturday's schedule," or "Welcome our newest instructor to the team" would be common posts for the local studio. Although these types of posts might help keep existing students up to date on what is happening, they certainly aren't the type of posts that someone is going to share; sharing with their circle of friends is the ultimate goal of social media marketing.

Therefore, it is critical that when using social media you make posts that:

- Are content rich. Ask yourself, "Would I want to share this with others?"

- Have some element of education, motivation, inspiration or humor.

- Ideally have an image or video attached to them to increase the appeal.

- When appropriate asks others to like or share.

- Have an outbound link that takes the person to an opt-in page that has a capture mechanism that is building one of your lists.

With an understanding of those basic rules and overall strategy, let's turn our discussion to the most popular social networks you should be considering.

FACEBOOK

As of this writing, Facebook is the largest and most popular social networking site. To anyone not already using it, perhaps it is best described as an online scrapbook of your life or business that also acts as a message board and personal communication tool. Facebook lets you upload photos and videos, establish groups and events, and communicate with any individual who "friends" you (a Facebook term meaning you've agreed to connect with that user). Facebook's multi-media format makes it incredibly viral; people like to know what others are doing—especially their friends.

Two other aspects to Facebook that dramatically increase its viral effectiveness are tags and comments. Users can attach names or key words to the content they post. For example, post a photo and "tag" the names of people in the photo, everyone who is a "friend" of those identified will get notified that your photo has been posted. This makes Facebook become something of an old-fashioned chain letter. Social networks are essentially open-source databases: By connecting with one, you potentially connect with many.

> The statistics for Facebook penetration are astounding.

The statistics for Facebook penetration are astounding. As of October, 2013, there are over 1.26 billion registered users. According to the company, in January of 2014 there were 757 million users that are active daily. It is estimated that 54% of all Americans currently have a Facebook "profile." Some other interesting statistics that the company reports: The average user spends 31 minutes per day on Facebook! (For comparison, the average time someone spends on a typical web page is less than a minute.) More than 250 million users currently access Facebook through their mobile devices. The average user has 200 friends and creates 90 new pieces of content every month.

Astonishing to many, the fastest-growing group to join Facebook is 50- to 60-year-olds. Millions of people use Facebook every day. That's why you need to be there, too.

As mentioned earlier, the key to making any social networking site into a business tool is using it as a driver to build lists. Most businesses fail to do this, using Facebook as just a message board for members. Entire books are dedicated to using Facebook in your business, here we are giving you a basic foundation and point you in the right direction.

FACEBOOK PAGES

As a Facebook user you must create a personal profile, which is, as it sounds, personal. If you own a business, you want customers to be connected to your company, not you personally. That's why

Facebook created what it calls "Pages." In business terms, Pages are like corporate entities or partnerships and were designed specifically for businesses, brands and celebrities interested in having large numbers of people following them or their products. But, before you can create a business Page you must have a personal profile.

It is vital that you create a Page for your business. One important reason is that Pages are search-engine optimized, while personal profiles are not. Every time you make a new posting to your Facebook Page, search engines note your new content and add it to the "web" of connections associated with your club, helping improve your rankings when anyone does a search.

Another reason is that Pages can host other social networking apps like a blog and Twitter. Connections between several social networking platforms help improve the optimization and "stickiness" of the content you post. Post something to your Facebook page and it's automatically posted to your blog (if you have one and have connected the two) and Twitter accounts. As each account grows in numbers, the more people will see your content—hence greater optimization.

A third good reason for using Facebook Pages is that they provide visitor statistics. By learning more about the profiles of those connected with you, you can make better decisions about content and marketing.

FACEBOOK GROUPS

This is another Facebook option that often causes confusion. As its name implies, a Group is like a social club of people with similar interests or causes. Often small business owners mistakenly create a Group under their business name instead of establishing a Page. But from a business perspective, this is a terrible decision.

A Page is seen as an entity, but a Group is connected to your personal profile. Therefore, if you created "ABC Yoga" as a Group, users can see only that it's connected to you personally. As a small, independent business operator, this may not seem like a bad thing initially, but there are limitations. The three primary benefits of Pages, as discussed earlier—SEO, hosting of other social media applications, and visitor statistics—are not available in Group usage. Also, you are limited to fewer than 5,000 Friends. This may not be important now but why limit yourself up front? You have no idea how successful your business may become or how many studio locations you may ultimately own!

For these reasons, Pages are commonly regarded as better suited for businesses, brands and celebrities, while Groups are best for organizing and interacting on a smaller scale. For example, if your studio has different types of classes or perhaps a yoga teacher's training program, using the Group feature would be appropriate. You have more control over who joins and can send messages directly to Group members. With Pages, you communicate through what's called a Wall, basically one big message board. Finally, Group members can send "join" invitations to their friends, another feature not available on Pages.

The bottom line is that both Pages and Groups are important; you just need to determine which is better for your business purposes.

FACEBOOK DRIVERS

The first thing that drives the success of your Facebook account—and probably No. #1 for all social networking—is useful, valuable, and interesting content. If you post only event messages and studio announcements, chances are prospects won't be interested. But if your content is interesting and entertaining, also related to yoga and wellness in general, your audience will grow—especially with new customers.

Another driver for Facebook success is leveraging the multi-media platform. In addition to posts that only contain writing, be sure to include some with pictures and video to engage people. If you use Facebook yourself, how much more time do you spend on someone's profile when they have lots of profile pictures and albums? You can lose all sense of time when watching videos—assuming they are interesting.

> *Media content becomes most powerful when you place "tags" on it.*

Media content becomes most powerful when you place "tags" on it. As mentioned earlier, you would "tag" a photo with the names of those pictured, resulting in all the individual's friends being notified that they've been "tagged." Add a description that subtly mentions where the photo was taken (the studio) and the occasion, and you have woven a very soft marketing element into that Facebook post. This information alone should motivate you to take photos and videos of your students at events and post them on your Pages!

A third driver, mentioned several times earlier, is connecting to other social networking platforms. "Cross links" are incredibly powerful, not only because they allow greater networking among users of these different networks, but also because they create a more links on the internet. More links makes search engines think you're more important. Luckily, most of the popular sites have tools, which make it simple to automatically create these cross links. For example, if you post a video on YouTube, you simply check a box on YouTube and the video will get posted to your Facebook Page simultaneously.

Finally, and most obvious, is the number of Likes you have. When someone "Likes" your business, anyone who visits their profile can see the name of that business. As with all marketing, it's a numbers game. Just as only a percentage of people will respond to an ad, only a certain percentage of people will note that their Friend has Liked your business or care about a posting where someone mentioned your class or studio. Therefore, the more Likes you have, the more people you can potentially reach. The real key is managing all three elements—(1) posting great content with tags and descriptors, (2) using multiple mediums, and (3) growing your number of Likes as a result.

FACEBOOK MISTAKES

Aside from poor content, not using multiple media to create interest, being too overt with promotions and not connecting to other social media platforms, here are four other common mistakes that will reduce the success of your Facebook activity. Some are more technical in nature, but use this list to locate more information in internet marketing publications or in a Google search.

- **Mistake #1:** *Not using tags when posting pictures and videos.* We have mentioned this already, but it's important to emphasize. A "tag" gives identifying words or names to pictures and video content you post. When you tag something posted on a Page, search engines will find and index that piece of content. Therefore, if you don't correctly tag your photos and videos with names and/or key words, you'll miss out on SEO opportunities.

- **Mistake #2:** *Not posting regularly.* For most small businesses this is by far the most difficult factor to monitor. You'll be busy with the day-to-day of operating your business and, unless you have someone dedicated to handle your social media, it's too easy for even weeks to pass without a new post. But search engines are mechanical and as such, they look for patterns. Certainly the more new content you post the better results you will get. However, it's actually more important to have consistent postings. Therefore, better to post once a week—like clockwork, on the same day, even at the same time—than to post sporadically and inconsistently. If you make a new posting every Tuesday at

8 AM (which you can use programs like www.facesoftware and www.ubotstudio), search engines will start to recognize this regularity and come sweep your site each week following that time.

- **Mistake #3:** *Not allowing comments or media posts from others.* It may seem a bit scary to open up your Facebook Page to any comments and posts, but this is what people on social networks have come to expect. Yes, you are vulnerable to negative posts. But if you do things right, the positive posts far outweigh the negative, which keep you on your toes.

- **Mistake #4:** *Not inviting people to your Facebook Page.* As part of our research process today, it's second nature for us to try and find the website of a company or product that interests us. The same is becoming true for Facebook Pages—as a consumer, we'll pull up a Facebook Page (or Google Review, Yelp or YellowPages) to see how many Likes they have and what the online banter is saying. You wouldn't dream of placing an ad without your website address on it, so do the same with your Facebook Page. Your Facebook link should appear on your website, your business cards, and all your marketing materials. Only by driving people to the Page will you grow your number of followers and Likes.

Facebook isn't leaving the social networking scene anytime soon. Of course, just before it arrived, writers may have said the same about MySpace. But today, Facebook reaches over a billion users at the whopping cost of free to consumers and businesses. Certainly monetary success takes the right strategy, time and patience. By providing great content and driving prospects to your list, you will begin to leverage the power of Facebook in your marketing.

YOUTUBE

As you probably know, YouTube is a video sharing social network site that lets people post videos for free. For most internet users, it's impossible to go online without thinking of YouTube. Yet YouTube only began in 2005! Today, in any 60-day period, more video content gets uploaded to YouTube than the three major U.S. television networks created in the last 60 years. The average YouTube user spends between 15 and 25 minutes a day on the site. As of September 2013, YouTube had over 1 million unique daily users worldwide.

> *The average YouTube user spends between 15 and 25 minutes a day on the site.*

It only makes sense that a video sharing site would have more traction than ones using only words and static pictures. Video is dynamic, much more personal and can entertain. Videos that go "viral," get millions of hits in a short period of time. These "viral" videos usually fall into two categories, with the funny outnumbering the inspirational by far.

THE PERSONALITY POWER OF VIDEO

From a business perspective, having a YouTube channel is somewhat like having your own television channel. Used correctly, video lets you be perceived as an expert if you can convey interesting, educational information. Another aspect is that video lets you connect deeper with your audience, who can see all your facial expressions and mannerisms—relatively unfiltered! If you have no desire to go on YouTube videos yourself, perhaps you can find someone else who wants to be the face behind your studio. The bottom line is that *if* you use video correctly, it will become a powerful tool to attract prospects and educate your students.

Video is equally effective in connecting with search engines. Post both a video and a printed article at the same time, and chances are that in today's SEO world, your video will get found more quickly and get more links and clicks. Google loves YouTube videos because Google OWNS YouTube. Of course they make sure content on one of their sites is at the top of any search list. That may change in the future but for now, take advantage of that and leverage the power of video.

> ...the best videos are like the best social media posts: informative and entertaining...

Remember that when using video to market your business, the best videos are like the best social media posts: informative and entertaining, rather than pushy or "salesy." In fact, YouTube has been known to suddenly and without notice close accounts of those businesses they feel are misusing YouTube and not providing useful information. Known as getting "Google-slapped", there doesn't seem to be a rhyme or reason – other than the videos were "too promotional" in nature and led to an entire account getting closed and all videos gone. Moral of the story (1) always back up your videos on your own computers and (2) keep your videos fun, interesting, educational, and entertaining, and you'll have viewers for years to come.

MAKING VIDEOS IS SIMPLE

With the introduction of USB cameras that integrate editing and uploading software, you can make and post a video on the internet in a matter of minutes. Cost for these cameras can range from around $49 to $249, making them affordable to anyone.

Of course, if you have any type of smart phone you can take hi-definition videos and upload them directly to YouTube without having to render them! You can edit directly on the iPhone or you can upload into a software program and edit. The only drawback with an iPhone is that there is no direct line for audio input, which means the sound quality might not be so good. The good news is that there is at least one product that turns an iPhone into a complete video camera with a tripod connector and an inline microphone. It is called the AR-4i by Fostex and costs around $99 on Amazon. No doubt there are similar devices for the most popular phones.

TIPS FOR SUCCESS

Many books, websites and even YouTube videos can teach you to shoot good video footage, so we won't dedicate much space to the subject. But to let you get started without delay, here are a few of the basics.

Distance. No matter what quality of camera you record with, uploading your finished product to YouTube modifies the size (hence quality) to permit smooth streaming. This always makes the video become slightly blurred compared to the original, so you must consider the distance from which you record your subject, particularly if someone is speaking. You don't want an ant-sized person on the screen too small for the viewer to see and connect with.

Lighting. Even worse than a tiny subject is a tiny subject in the dark. Unfortunately, this happens with a lot of "home" produced videos shot indoors without the benefit of professional lighting. Some of the very best videos are shot outside during the day. Although outdoors may not be ideal for shooting yoga poses, it could be a good solution for some of your personal video messages. Along with good natural lighting, outdoor backgrounds can be more interesting than white walls. For videos that focus on yoga poses, try for a location with good overhead lighting or consider purchasing a professional lighting kit, which starts around $200. Canister and track lights will almost always leave shadows on your face.

Sound. One benefit of the newer USB cameras is a port for a line-feed microphone—which is also an option of higher-quality video cameras. When your camera has this feature, make sure you use it. You can purchase an inexpensive lavaliere microphone (also known as a "lav" or lapel microphone) and long cord for less than $25. Nothing is more annoying than watching a video whose audio quality is so poor that you find yourself trying to lip read or having to replay it. In fact, to many viewers, good sound is more important than a good picture. If you're using a camera with no audio input, make sure that you are shooting close enough to the subject that spoken words are clearly recorded.

THREE MORE OPTIONS FOR GREAT VIDEO.

If the thought of creating your own video sends you into child's pose, we would like to offer you three viable alternatives for getting great video.

1. There is probably someone in your classes or a member of you studio who is handy with a video camera who would like to help you for a small fee or on an exchange/trade basis.

2. Contact your local colleges. They might have students in a video or communication arts program that need a class project and would gladly take on your work for free. You might also find an intern with these skills.

3. Set a budget and put an advertisement up on Craig's List. You will get tons of videographers looking for work!

TEST RUN

Regardless of what camera you use or who is shooting, when getting started it is always best to perform a 20-second shoot of your intended subject, in the exact location you'll use, at the estimated distance. Then either load that short video onto a computer to watch it or better yet, upload it to YouTube and be certain of how it will look as a finished product.

Certainly there are other video social network sites, like Vimeo, and we are not suggesting you shouldn't use them. What we do know is that as a small business operator it is challenging enough to get your videos made and up on the most popular video site. So, once you have mastered YouTube by all means look to other ways in which you can leverage your videos and get more views and opt-ins!

A FEW LAST WORDS ON YOU TUBE

When you finally load your finished video to YouTube, be sure to let the world know about it. Announce it on all your social media, in your blog and in your newsletters. Also when selecting a You Tube channel for the first time you will be asked to create a name – while it is tempting to use your studios name make sure the title of your channel includes a search term that people might use for searching for your services like "yoga"!

Keep in mind that in addition to being huge repository for video, YouTube is also a search engine and acts like one. You will be asked to enter a description and key words when you upload your video. Remember, keywords are words or short phrases that someone would use when searching for your services or products. These should also be sprinkled into your description.

TWITTER

Twitter is actually considered a micro-blogging social network because entries cannot exceed 140 characters of plain text. A link is the only way to add video or pictures. Many people don't understand the big hype around Twitter and thought that "Tweeting" (Twitter-ese for posting a message) would not survive. Boy, were they wrong. Twitter is one of the top networking sites and therefore, you need to be aware of it and utilize it if you can.

Twitter was introduced to the world in March of 2006. As of September, 2013, Twitter had over 1 billion accounts. Over 100 million Tweets are posted on Twitter every day, and its search engines get 600 million daily queries. Perhaps most significant is that 75% of all Twitter traffic comes from *outside* Twitter.com— which testifies to the viral nature of Tweets.

If you had to explain Twitter to a grandmother, you might say that it's one big chat room with an endless number of people all posting short messages (under 140 characters) that range from whatever they are doing at the moment to "teaser" comments that include links to a blog, video, photo or some other online resource. That may be an oversimplification, but that's what Twitter basically is: random thoughts by a mishmash of people who are connected only through their connections with others!

WHY USE TWITTER?

As chaotic as the site may sound, there are reasons why Twitter can be such a powerful marketing tool. First, messages are 100% deliverable. If anyone has opted to "Follow" you, whenever you Tweet a message, it will be displayed in that person's timeline, displayed in real time on their Twitter home page. Of course, Twitter is not like email where the person opens a message; so whether they actually see or read that Tweet will depend upon their patterns of use. What you do know, however, is that the message was delivered to their Twitter time line.

> *...messages are 100% deliverable.*

Another element that makes Twitter so powerful is that any user can see the name and profile of any other user, making Twitter an amazing open-source database. If I want to sell a product or service to triathletes, I can click on profiles that mention triathlons and determine whether or not to follow them. Or I could search for businesses that cater to triathletes, see all of their followers and, once again, choose to follow them. Once you are following someone, chances are they'll check out your profile and, in return, and Follow you. Twitter gives you access to virtually every user out there, and the ability to reach an unlimited number of potential prospects.

Yes, using Twitter may take some time and effort, but never forget that this is all available to your business for zero dollars. Your only investment is time. And, you can utilize automation software that sends out your Tweets at specified times, and will post the Tweet to your other social networking sites. For those of you who can embrace and stay organized with your technology—Twitter can become a positive marketing medium.

CONSIDER THE POSSIBILITIES

Suppose you decided your local sports shop would be a perfect joint marketing partner and asked them for their database so you could approach their customers. Most likely, they would tell you "No." Alternatively, you can simply go onto that business' Twitter account to see who's following them. That might not be an exact match of their customer base, but it would give you a list of individuals interested in sports products and services. Just by following those individuals, you have complete access to them.

Another example of how Twitter can be used is networking with your students who are influencers. In the Twitter world an "influencer" is someone who has a large number of people following them. Let's suppose that one of your students is an influencer. You can work out an arrangement with them to hold a "Tweetup," which refers to a person inviting their followers to an event or happening via a Tweet.

> " *Another example of how Twitter can be used is networking with your students who are influencers.*

Imagine an influencer holding a "Lunchtime Yoga Tweetup" at your studio and including a link to a class pass? Even if only a few showed up, consider the number of people who could have seen the invitation! Not only could this result in potential new students but the value in the influencer's endorsement and top of mind awareness is considerable—and free. Of course, you could establish monthly or quarterly events with those influencers who get results. The possibilities are only limited to your creativity and organizational skills.

One big advantage of Twitter is the ability to direct the viewer anywhere, using a link. Therefore, if you want people to watch a YouTube video, you would make a short post that enticed them to click the link, which brings them to the video. If you want them to check out a blog or a photo, you would do the same thing, perhaps directing them to your Pinterest account (discussed later).

People expect Tweets to direct them to other sites. Yes, your short message must engage them somewhat, but that's all part of the fun of making it work.

HASHTAGS AREN'T FOR BREAKFAST

One final item to mention is the use of hashtags (a hashtag looks like this: #). Hashtags are used by those making a Tweet to mark phrases, keywords or names, which make it easier for people to filter through the millions of searches. For example, suppose you were having a 30 Days of Yoga program and you called it "The 30 Day Challenge." Anytime you make a Tweet about this topic you would use #30DayChallenge. It might look like this:

"See this week's body transformation at #30DayChallenge."

The biggest advantage to the hashtag is that someone who is following this topic can click on the hashtag word and find all other Tweets that have utilized the exact same wording. From a marketing perspective this makes it easier for you to maintain interest with followers of this topic. Hashtags that become very popular actually become "trending topics" on Twitter. Although it would be highly unlikely that your studio or 30 day challenge would become a trend, you might be able to pick up broader exposure by making # Tweets on a trending topic. If your comment and subsequent content is interesting and/or valuable it could get the attention of new followers.

The good and bad news about Twitter is that it's simple. Unlike Facebook, with its many different navigation pages, Twitter is very straightforward, easier to use and manage. You have your profile and your timeline—that's it. On the other hand, its' very simplicity makes it more challenging because you have to be more creative to grab attention.

As with other social networks, you should invest in books and resources that give you the information and training you need to take full advantage of Twitter's great business applications. Specifically, online tools like Hootsuite.com and Monitter. com will help manage keep you organized and are great time saver when it comes to social media. We highly recommend that you use them.

LINKEDIN

LinkedIn is a business oriented social networking site designed to connect professionals, and is not focused on sharing content, however there are opportunities for this. Think of it is an online résumé combined with professional networking. Members of LinkedIn post their "profile," which includes their education, present and past job experience and affiliated associations or organizations. There is also a place where the member can have others recommend them. From an individual users perspective, LinkedIn's two big advantages are the users "connections" and its ability to create Groups within LinkedIn users.

Connections are those with whom the user has some sort of professional relationship, either personally or through six degrees of separation. Creating Groups allow users to find and attract others with similar professional interests. For example, as an instructor you may start a group targeted towards professionals who want to use yoga for stress reduction. You could use the Group platform feature to alert them of meetings or training activities. You could also attract and engage others by posting some content, although each group has its own rules regarding this.

LinkedIn also has direct ads to attract new customers. Businesses report that by creating a company profile on LinkedIn, similar to creating a Business Page on Facebook, they have generated prospects and sales. A company profile lets customers connect with the business and of course, make recommendations. Making regular "status updates" to your company's profile keeps customers up to date on any new products, services and employment opportunities.

Despite the endless possibilities for company profile connections, the challenge for most small business owners is time. Pay attention to LinkedIn only after your other consumer orientated marketing strategies are working to potential.

That said, it's easy for you to go create both a personal and a company profile on LinkedIn and simply react to others reaching out and connecting. More active users (in particular your students who frequently use LinkedIn) will find you, send you requests to connect, and eventually you will gain a decent number of connections.

GOOGLE+

Google+ is a social networking site that competes with Facebook. It was originally launched as a "by invitation only" and ended up gaining 10 million people in just a few days. That is the fastest membership growth of any social network—even Facebook. Similar to Facebook, Google + has both personal and business pages.

Google+ allows you to manage your connections more narrowly, into what they call "Circles." This means that you create sub-groups (Circles) of friends; Best friends, immediate family, extended family, work friends, college friends, etc., and that you control the information going to each Circle.

> *...the Circles feature was originally utilized for personal use, its application to business is powerful.*

Although the Circles feature was originally utilized for personal use, its application to business is powerful. Think about it: you can now organize your fans and followers in different categories. This allows you to customize the information you send out to each group.

Circles is only one of the features in an entire suite of social tools on Google+. Another important feature is Hangouts. We mentioned these during our discussion of capture mechanisms. Hangouts are live-streaming video where you can have multiple people visible to the audience that is watching. If you were to get really creative, Hangouts could give you the ability to offer classes as "at home workouts." Imagine being able to work with students via video and still see them performing their postures as they were coached through the routine. Pretty powerful.

The "What's Hot" feature of Google + is a content-creating dream for small business operators. Remember that for any social networking site to gain search engine optimization you need to be posting regular content. This proves problematic for most small business people who don't have time to constantly create content. The "What's Hot" feature allows you to identify the most recommended and shared items happening on Google + and then share that information on your own page. When you combine this feature with Circles, it allows you to share specific content to particular circles, making you look like a genius who knows what kind of information their students want.

To the layperson, Google Authorship is a service provided through Google + that allows you to manage your identity and brand on the internet by connecting the original content you create to your avatar photo and byline within your Google + account. No doubt you have seen this when you perform a Google search; where some postings come up with a video snippet connecting to YouTube while others come up with a small picture of the author. The latter is the result of Google Authorship.

From a more technical perspective, Google Authorship is designed to help Google manage credible sources and give expert authors higher ranks over advertisements on search results. Basically Google wants searchers to do less digging through junk to find the content they are searching for.

There are several reasons you should want to take advantage of Google Authorship. First of all the obvious visual identity means that a searcher will be connected to your photo. If you are truly an expert in the field this means your face will come up consistently, helping you to build a stronger brand. Second, Google gives more weight to content that has been authored because they can verify it; higher rank means you will get noticed more quickly. Third is credibility; people are more apt to believe the content when they connect with a person and not a bunch of words.

For all these reasons you should really begin using Google Authorship. Obviously, you need a Gmail address to have a Google + account and it is within Google + that you will have the option to register for authorship. Simply Google, "Setting up Google Authorship" to find the most recent instructions.

Google reaches over 1 billion unique visitors each month making it the number one internet site. Gaining exposure is the number one obstacle in marketing. Obviously this isn't an issue for Google so utilizing Google + should be on your list of options to explore.

PINTEREST

Pinterest is another of the newer social networking sites that allows users to let their friends know what things they find interesting by pinning them to what are called "boards" on their site. Hence the name Pinterest—"pinning your interests."

For people who are very visual this is a social networking dream come true because aside from giving a name to each of your online boards, there is no typing involved! In essence it is one huge personal scrapbook. Imagine you find a recipe online that you love. There is a picture of the finished dish. You can simply use their tool to "pin" that picture, post it into one of your boards named "recipes to try and voila, there it sits in your account. Now it's easy for you to go back and find the recipe when you're ready to try it. Further, any friends that you are connected with can view the recipe as well. Of course, Pinterest incorporates both Facebook and Twitter, making the viral sharing potential incredible.

You may be thinking to yourself, "Why the heck is Pinterest being included in a business book?" Well, there are some very interesting potential business applications with this social network site. This type of site fits perfectly into the entire concept of internet marketing that we have been advocating; not pro-actively selling but sharing interests and information with others. If you can make something interesting—whether it be a photo of the right pose or a video explaining something about a yoga practice—the potential for others to Pin your content to their board is a winner.

Imagine that you create a number of 3-5 minute yoga for stress relief videos. These would be poses that someone could easily do at work or quickly at home. You could have a contest on your website where you ask people to vote on their favorite and then encourage them to Pin that video to their Pinterest account. The "Pin It" widget makes this simple and easy to do. You may think this all sounds farfetched but people love this kind of stuff—especially women—and they the primary audience for every yoga class!

ONLINE COUPON PROGRAMS

No marketer could have predicted that businesses would line up to offer customers 50% off *and* that the business would only receive half of money collected—bringing their revenue to 25% of the retail "value." One of the most popular online coupon companies, Groupon, keeps half of money collected from each buyer. Despite this, online coupons have now become the rage. This has been partly fueled by the economic recession and partly by the power of social networking. Groupon offers "daily deals" on things to see, do, eat and buy in over 400 markets and thousands of cities around the world.

Their original concept was for businesses to post an awesome daily deal, only if a minimum number of consumers agreed to buy in. This fueled early adopters to share their deals with friends, encouraging them to buy and obtain the minimum. Groupon has become so successful that they no longer have minimums and many deals are offered each day. The company encourages users to refer friends by offering the person who gave the referral to earn $10 in "Groupon Bucks."

Today, although the initial frenzy has worn off, Groupon has millions subscribers. The most frequent users seem to be in major metropolitan areas, but Groupon has expanded into smaller cities. After the Groupon explosion, dozens of other online coupon programs sprung up but many have fallen by the wayside. Two popular US coupon programs that have survived are Living Social and Amazon Local. Internationally there are many others, as well as smaller programs in local communities.

Only time will tell, but the online coupon craze seems to have changed how consumers now buy. People expect ridiculously low offers to coax them through the doors of a business.

> *... coupon programs have changed the way businesses market themselves.*

In addition, coupon programs have changed the way businesses market themselves. First, businesses are willing to accept 25% of the retail value of an offering. Second, they now get paid to advertise! Think about the process. The coupon company sends out an advertisement to thousands of subscribers who have asked to be marketed to. This costs the business nothing except the agreement to provide the coupon company with a great deal. In exchange they are going to get paid for all coupons purchased—even if the consumer doesn't use the promotion.

Of course, businesses must carefully think through the type of offer they want to make, ensuring that a promotion won't put them out of business. But so long as a coupon program is done right, this is a wonderful, risk-free marketing tool.

COUPON POSSIBILITIES

In one scenario, you offer a 30-day, 10-visit class pass (which has to be used within 30 days of activation). Retail value: $150. Groupon requires you offer the deal at a minimum of half off, which would be $75. You split the revenue with Groupon, receiving a total of $37.50 per sale. For this to be a sound business decision, you must be able to give up those mat spots over the next month knowing you will only get $37.50, *and/or* you need to ensure that trying out your classes will ultimately convert into a long-term student.

It sounds simple enough but there is some complexity to it. You need to make sure you have the space, you can afford to lose the cash flow for a period of time and that you won't upset your current student base. This can be dangerous for studios that are already up and running but is a possible winning strategy for a new studio. Let's give a non-yoga studio example to better make the point regarding coupons being potentially dangerous marketing.

Second scenario: You are a pizza shop, selling large cheese pizzas for normally $15. Your Groupon coupon lets consumers buy a pizza for $7.50, and after splitting the money, you collect a grand total of $3.75 per pizza. Given the actual costs of material and labor, you aren't likely to break even. (Be aware that existing customers will use the coupons too. You must have cash on hand to float any short-term losses). But if you think it's worth it to attract new customers *then* it's worth a try. Businesses that go into the promotion with a long-term strategy to convert Groupon users to customers can make it profitable.

KEY COUPON STRATEGIES

We suggest that you explore any and all online coupon programs but keep these important strategic points in mind:

- Think through what type of product or service you plan to offer! Typically you'll receive only 25% of its retail value.

- Make sure you can fulfill consumers' demand without bankrupting your studio.

- To ensure success, focus on two parameters: (1) Hard-labor costs to deliver the purchase can't exceed the cash you collect from the deal. (2) "Back-end sales," or additional purchases by your new Groupon customers, will occur after they've been exposed to your business.

- If possible, include some kind of opt-in (you want to get email addresses) on your coupon offer to include an online bonus. For Groupon deals, the show-up ratio is often low. An additional opt-in offer will help draw more prospects into your database, even if they don't redeem the deal.

- Focus on back-end sales! Don't be greedy up front and use the coupon as a bait-and-switch. This makes for bad P.R. and is sure to backfire.

- Be prepared for an influx of Groupon students, which could stress some businesses. Make sure customers have a positive experience that will result in future business for you.

- Before you run the coupon, have a conversion strategy in place. This means having a strategy for turning that class pass into a long-term student.

By taking time to make these calculations you will be better positioned to formulate the right offer for success.

MAKING SOCIAL MEDIA MARKETING WORK

All your online efforts have one ultimate goal: to generate a huge database of interested prospects, build trust with them, and ultimately get them to take some action. When done right that action is visiting your studio or taking a class. To accomplish this goal, all your social marketing efforts must lead fans, followers, connections and viewers to a web page that exposes them to some sort of capture mechanism. That mechanism should entice them to opt-in without hard-selling them. Never expect most to opt-in, but those you successfully entice will be that many more in your database, where you have the chance to earn their business.

> *...all your social marketing efforts must lead fans, followers, connections and viewers to a web page that exposes them to some sort of capture mechanism.*

Entire books are dedicated to using social networking in business. You could buy one that focuses entirely on Facebook, another just for Twitter, so do continue your internet marketing education, focusing on areas you've determined will bring you the most success. We recommend that you jump in where you are most interested, remembering it takes time to become familiar with each.

Also, it is important to remember that the social media space changes at light speed. What is the latest and greatest today may be obsolete in a matter of months. Therefore, it is important that you stay on top of what is new.

CHAPTER 8

INCREASING FREQUENCY OF VISITS AND LOYALTY

The first half of this book has primarily focused on marketing efforts to grow the student base of your classes. Obviously, without enough students your classes and/or studio won't be profitable enough to stay in business. Therefore, it makes sense that much of your time, energy and marketing budget will go towards new student acquisition.

However, as we discussed in Chapter 1, "getting new customers" is only one of the three ways to grow revenue in your business. In this chapter we will turn our discussion to the topic of increasing the frequency of student visits, their spending, and building loyalty.

TO DISCOUNT OR NOT?

When giving seminars and asking the attendees "What is one way in which you can get your students to come more often," the most common answer we get is "Discount the class price." That is a natural reaction for many because we are wired as consumers to associate a discount with more spending. When it comes to building your yoga practice, though, that is flawed reasoning. For one, the difference between $12 per class and $15 per class isn't enough of a motivating factor for most people to get themselves to an extra class a week. For the average "mainstream" yoga student who participates in two classes per week, it is finding (justifying) the time to fit in another class, not the price difference.

> *...discounting for higher per-student usage could actually result in a significant loss of revenue.*

Second, and perhaps more important from a business operator's perspective, discounting for higher per-student usage could actually result in a significant loss of revenue. The reason is that very often the people who take advantage of discount packages or class packs are the very students who would have come more often anyways. Let's show this by way of example.

To keep it simple, let's suppose you have 25 students. 20% of them (5) attend class 4 times per week (the "serious" students) and the other 80% are mainstream and attend twice a week. Your day rate is $15 per class. 20 students x $15 = $300 x twice weekly = $600 in revenue. 5 students x $15 = $75 x four times weekly = $300 in revenue. This brings the total weekly revenue of all the students to $900. If you offered discount class packs where anyone could buy ten classes at the discounted rate of $12 (just an example), the difference could be substantial.

It would be safe to assume that those taking 4 classes per week would all purchase the discounted packages. Therefore, 5 students x $12 = $60 x four times weekly = $240 in revenue. Further, let's assume that only half of the other students wanted to buy the discounted package (some might not have the $120 to buy the package and others just might not care). So, 10 students x $15 = $150 x twice weekly = $300 in revenue. Then, 10 students at $12 = $120 x twice weekly = $240 in revenue. The total of those three different groups is now $780, not $900. That is a difference of $120 per week or $480 per month. That could potentially be a difference of $5,760 per year—and that was using an example of just 25 students.

Whether you agree with those numbers or not doesn't matter. The point is that it is very easy to initially decide, "I'm going to offer a discounted pack of classes to help increase usage," without really thinking through the financial implications. Furthermore, until you have enough history with student usage patterns it is very challenging to figure out what price breaks may or may not influence the number of classes students participate in per week.

We are NOT saying that you should never discount. Rather, we are saying that you must make such decisions based on a) a full understanding of the usage patterns of your student population and b) a complete analysis of revenue shifts that could take place. Once you are fully informed and educated then and only then can you make a good business decision. And, given that this one decision can have such a huge impact on your financial success it should not be made in haste. That said, the remainder of this chapter will turn our focus away from price and discuss creative strategies and ideas that can increase the frequency of class uses by your students.

FREQUENT PARTICIPANT INCENTIVES

Have you even noticed that with many things in life you work the hardest for the silliest things? You and your friends complete a grueling obstacle course so you can have the T-shirt that tells the world you "did it"—even when you paid for participating. Or, spend a ridiculous amount of money (and time) at the carnival to win a cheap teddy bear because you want your kid to walk around with the prize. What the fitness industry has discovered over the years is that people know they should exercise; what they need is motivation.

Let's suppose that the average student at your studio attends 8 classes per month. If you could bump that up to 10 uses per month, that would mean an extra $30 per month or $360 per year PER student. So, we're not talking about a huge difference in usage for the individual but the result is a substantial difference in revenue.

Imagine that you created a program whereby any student who attended 10 or more classes per month would a) get a special discount coupon for something at a popular local business and b) would be entered into a drawing to win a gift card to that same business. Sounds too simple but it works great in the fitness industry. It is called the Frequent Sweater's Club and it's simple to do. The owner of the fitness facility establishes relationships with local businesses whereby once a year that "partner" would be featured to the members of the club.

Let's suppose you are going to work with a local restaurant. The restaurant supplies your business with a discount coupon for all the students who participate in 10 or more classes that month. It might be for a percentage discount or maybe something free, like an appetizer with the purchase of an entrée. In addition they provide you with a $50 gift card. You promote that business all month long to your students. Assuming you partner with businesses that are popular and in demand, students will try harder to meet the 10 class minimum a) just to get the coupon and b) for a chance to win the gift card.

Of course, not all your students will be interested in every single promotion but if you can increase class participation by 15 or 20% each month that will result in a significant increase in revenue over the course of a year! Best of all, aside from organizing the promotion it costs you nothing. With a little creativity and some solid networking with the local businesses in your area this can become a very popular program at your studio.

For those of you asking yourself, "But why would a local business want to do this for me?" the answer is "They are doing it for themselves!" If you have a decent student population and there is a good match between your demographics and their customers it is a no brainer for the business. For a very nominal cost they now have the opportunity to drive more customers through their doors. Just the promotion alone that will happen through your internal marketing posters and signs will be of value to a local business.

> " *For a very nominal cost they now have the opportunity to drive more customers through their doors.*

EDUCATION INFLUENCES USAGE

One of the most interesting things about human beings is their predictability when it comes to behavioral change. This discussion about finding ways to increase class participation falls into the category of behavioral change. The reality is that we are trying to get an individual to change the priorities in their life so they will dedicate more time and money to coming to yoga classes.

Regardless of whether or not a person is trying to change a habit by adding something (more exercise) or removing something (stop smoking), the stages of change they will go through are identical. They are:

- *Pre-contemplation;* the person isn't even aware that they should change. Therefore there is no desire to change. Until something happens that makes them aware of the need the thought to change won't cross their mind.

- *Contemplation;* the person becomes aware of the need to change but their state of mind is "I should do that." Therefore the desire to change is not strong enough to take action. Someone could be in the contemplation stage for a long time unless something happens to move them into the next stage.

- *Preparation;* the person's level of desire has become greater. They begin to say to themself, "I am going to do this." The time it takes them to move from this stage to the next can vary greatly from hours to months, even years.

- *Action;* the person actually starts (or stops) the behavior. For example, they buy the yoga program or they smoke the last cigarette in the pack and resolve to not buy another. Once someone takes action they immediately move onto the next stage.

- *Maintenance;* the person has to consciously work at maintaining their new behavior. It is effort for them at this stage.

- *Termination;* the person totally integrates their new behavior without the risk of falling back into old habits. Therefore, when they go away on vacation they find the closest yoga studio so they don't have to miss class. Alternatively, they are never tempted to smoke a cigarette again and won't allow anyone to smoke in their car or house.

To bring all this information back to the discussion of increasing class participation, for someone to move from one stage to the next one of two things needs to happen. Either they need to have a significant emotional experience or they need to be educated. An example of the former would be going to put on your shorts for the first time after winter and you can't button them. The alarm bells go off in your head, "Oh, I better do something about this." The latter, education, might happen if you read an article in your favorite health and fitness magazine that talked about the benefits of yoga for low back pain sufferers.

> " *Either they need to have a significant emotional experience or they need to be educated.*

As marketers we are not in control of when an individual has a significant emotional experience. As a result, in order to get someone to make a change we must educate them. The consumer must know why it is beneficial for them to come to more yoga classes per week—specifically. Sure, they may know logically that if they exercised more they would get greater benefits but that in and of itself is not enough to get them to change.

One poster that was very effective at educating participants had a list of all the benefits of exercising and then three columns to the right entitled "1-2 times per week, "3-5 times per week" and "6-7 times per week." Of course, the column that showed 6-7 times per week had every benefit checked off. As subtle as the poster was, simply being displayed at this fitness facility, it subconsciously made its point loud and clear.

We are not suggesting that you need to make posters that outline the benefits of yoga (but it's a good idea if you decide to do it). What we are suggesting is that you must provide your students with on-going education about the benefits of yoga. Post articles that appear in yoga magazines or other publications. Find links online to articles and even YouTube videos that you can share. One very successful retailer in Connecticut had a slogan, "An educated consumer is our best customer." The very same concept holds true for increasing the number of class visits that your students make. How might you educate your students?

- Flyers

- Brochures

- Posters

- Online articles

- Your newsletter or blog

- During class

- Special workshops

- Magazine articles reprinted

- Books

EVERYONE LIKES A LITTLE MOTIVATION!

Another key aspect to behavioral change is motivation. Certainly when you educate people you will accomplish some motivation but the best way to compliment your education is through inspirational testimonials. Feature short stories or quotes by your students who tell their personal story about how their life was transformed by increasing the number of yoga classes they do each week. People like education but they get inspired when they read stories about "regular" people who have made positive changes. Further, if you can establish a good number of stories that represent a wide variety of people you will ensure that there is a relatable story for every type of student.

Finally, try to bring motivational quotes, posters and other images into your classroom or studio. Most people respond well to visual images and everyone wants a little pick me up to their environment. We have visited one studio that had a flat screen in the entrance area with inspiring quotes and images that scrolled continuously. This was a very nice touch. Another studio had a photographer come in and take pictures of the students in class. The shots were done in black and white with interesting angles and filters, and some of the images were intentionally made a bit blurry to accentuate the depth. These were enlarged and framed and put up in the studio. Wow! What a great way to pay a compliment to students (assuming you have their permission). The result was interesting and personal artwork that was attractive and certainly unique.

This is certainly not an exhaustive list of ways to increase the number of monthly student visits but it provides you with some basic strategies and should get you thinking of other ways that you can implement yourself. The key is to always be watching the numbers and measuring whether or not what you are doing is actually having a positive influence on usage. We will dedicate a later chapter on specific KPI's (key performance indicators) that you should be tracking. Average number of monthly visits is one of the important statistics.

CHAPTER 9
INCREASE STUDENT SPENDING

It's now time to turn to the third way to grow revenue in any business; increasing the size of a customer's purchase. There are three basic strategies that can be used to increase the size of a customer's purchase. They are creating additional profit centers, cross-sells and up-sells.

A cross-sell is when the customer is asked to buy something related to the current purchase they are making. If you go into a store to buy a suit the clerk will always ask you if you need shirts, ties or socks. These would be cross-sells. An up-sell is when you are given the opportunity to buy more or a higher quality level of the item you are purchasing. Staying with the suit example you might be given a deal to buy two suits or the clerk may encourage you to upgrade to a better quality fabric, hence higher cost.

The most famous consumer business that has done a miraculous job at both of these strategies is McDonald's. When they first began real growth back in the 1970's they began asking their customers, "Would you like fries with that?" It seems like such a simple, no-brainer thing to do . . . in retrospect! No other retail food establishment had made this part of their protocol. What McDonald's soon realized was that upwards of 30% of customers would just say "Yes" simply when asked. No strong incentive or pushing from the clerk.

We don't want to date ourselves too much, but if we are remembering correctly, the cost for a small French fry at this time was around .30 cents. All food establishments work off of a minimum of 100% markup. That means that there was a .15 cent profit in every single one of these purchases. Making the math easy let's assume that the average store had 1,000 transactions a day that could be appropriately cross-sold to French fries. That would mean about 300 people PER DAY were accepting the offer. That means the profit was of a minimum of $45. Doesn't sound like much profit but now multiply that by 365 days! That's $16,425. To put that in perspective, the median household income in 1970 was around $9,700.

Now fast forward to the late 1980's. McDonald's became masters at the up-sell with the "super-size" concept. They made it easy to super-size your fries or your drink for a small additional cost, which was very enticing to consumers. "Wow, I can get an extra-large fry for just .30 cents more!" It was a huge hit. Of course, the additional cost of the extra fries or the additional soda was pennies, making these up-sells highly profitable.

If you remember back to our discussion on exponential results, increasing the cross-sell by 30% and the up-sell by 30% creates a compounding impact on revenue. Today every retailer tries to up-sell, cross-sell and bundle something; some to the point of aggravation. Suffice it to say that businesses wouldn't do it if it didn't work! The only question you need to ask is, "How can I apply these strategies to my business?" Below are some ideas.

> *Today every retailer tries to up-sell, cross-sell and bundle something...*

RETAIL PURCHASES

Perhaps one of the greatest overlooked source of revenue for yoga teachers and studios are retail purchases. Let's face it, students need and want various products to support their practice. According to a 2012 Yoga Journal study 20.4 million Americans practice yoga and spend $10.3 billion a year on yoga classes and products, including equipment, clothing, vacations, and media (DVDs, CD's). All indications are that this number will continue to trend upwards.

Keep in mind that your students will purchase yoga related products either from you or will look to other sources. Beyond the profit motives, there are a couple good reasons to offer students products they need. First, as a yoga professional you know what products are the best for your students. You are in the best position to make sure they get the items that will best serve their practice. Secondly, when you offer products that people need and want, you provide them with a valuable service and their relationship to you is deepened.

This may seem obvious, but it is amazing how many teachers we meet who are not offering these basic items to their students:

- Mats

- Blankets

- Bolsters

- Blocks

- Straps

- Books

- DVDs

- CDs

Let's do the math. Say that you sold only 1 of each of the items listed above each week and the average profit on per sale was $10; that would be $80 or $4,160 for the year. If you own a studio, you will easily sell much more.

We know of a yoga studio whose facility offers over 100 yoga classes a week and the owner has told us that studio makes more money from retail sales than the actual classes. Think about it!

Here are some additional items that are a natural to offer your students:

- Mat bags

- Meditation cushions

- Sandbags

- Eye pillows

- Essential oils

- Yoga clothing: shirts/t-shirts, pants, shorts, etc.

- Yoga related jewelry

- Posters

- Towels

- Water bottles

- Ayurvedic supplies

- Nutritional supplements

Many of the above items can be private labeled and branded with your studio's logo or message. Students love branded apparel so if you have the ability (and desire) to get shirts and sweatshirts made they add a nice touch to your offering. Furthermore, branded clothing is a fantastic way to get free advertising. We have had many people show up at our classes saying they initially discovered us because they saw someone with a "Let's Do Yoga" brand shirt on!

ONLINE PURCHASES

There will be many of you that like the idea of generating additional revenue from retail sales but may not have the space. For others you may just not want to deal with the purchasing and inventory issues that come with retail selling. Technology offers you the ability to make retail purchases without having to have any inventory!

> *" ... many retail product companies that offer what are called affiliate programs.*

First, there are many retail product companies that offer what are called affiliate programs. Basically this means that you promote a product or service via a link the company provides you. Anyone that clicks that link is tracked to you and a commission is generated. This could be something as small as 5% but, in the case of some services, can be upwards of 35%. Not bad for simply referring a product or service that you believe in. Here are few companies to check out:

- Cafepress.com

- Greenaffiliateprogams.net

- Yogaaccessories.com

- Barefootyoga.com

- Theultimateyogi.com

Another type of online revenue generator from retail sales of products is through what is called direct sales. This is very popular with natural health care product companies. The difference is that instead of becoming an affiliate, you become a wholesale distributor for the product line. Typically you would display promotional materials about the products in the studio and, when appropriate, have some of the product packaging displayed. For example, if you were promoting supplements you might display some empty bottles along with the brochures so that people will notice them and at least pick up the educational materials. Similar to an affiliate program, you typically have some kind of link to a website or member number that is listed on all your promotional materials. When the student goes online to purchase something they use the link or member number tracked back to you. Each month you have sales you get a check in the mail! Some studio operators are very successful with these types of programs and their income can become significant.

Given the type of market yoga studios attract, some of the more popular items that would fall into direct sales would include vitamins & minerals, whole food supplements, herbal supplements, organic personal care products, organic household cleaning products and one of our favorites, essential oils. There are many companies and products to choose from and what is important is that you find a line that a) is in alignment with a yogic lifestyle (all natural); b) is something that you believe in and personally advocate, and; c) has a good referral compensation program.

If you would like to know who we recommend as an ideal fit for this type of ancillary revenue stream in your business, see the information on page 00 in the back of this book.

WORKSHOPS, INTENSIVES, PRIVATE SESSIONS, AND SPECIAL CLASS SERIES

Aside from regular yoga classes you can offer *workshops* that focus on specific aspects of yoga. This can provide students with a deeper experience of yoga than they normally get in classes. You can charge anywhere from $25 to $125 or more per person, per workshop depending on the subject and length. Workshops can also be promoted to those outside of your studio as way of bringing new people into your facility.

Some popular topics include: Yoga philosophy and history, meditation, pranayama inversions, backbends, restorative yoga, yoga for men, prenatal and postnatal yoga, yoga for flexibility, yoga for back care, yoga for tight shoulders, partner yoga; the list goes on and on. You can ask your teachers for ideas too – they most likely will have many and be excited to help! Remember, you can always reach out to teachers who do not instruct at your studio that have special skills or areas of expertise.

Intensives are like workshops only longer: for a day, weekend, or week. Subject matter and focus can be the same as for workshops or you can combine various subjects for a theme such as wellness, flexibility, strength, weight loss, deepening your practice, etc. Obviously you would charge more for intensives than for workshops because of the longer class times and instruction.

Class series can also have a special theme and focus, such as; strength, abdominal work, balance, meditation, inversions, back care, philosophy, etc. These classes can be scheduled over a period of weeks or months and can command a special fee as they are separate from regular classes.

To find out what workshops, intensives, or class series your students would be most interested in attending, consider creating a simple interest form that you can post on your web site or pass out at the end of classes to get feedback.

If you are not running workshops, intensives and special class series, you are missing a great revenue opportunity as well missing the mark when it comes to helping your students deepen their practice and knowledge of yoga.

> *Private sessions can also be a great source of additional revenue...*

Private sessions can also be a great source of additional revenue and a terrific way to help people with yoga by being able to focus on the specific needs of the individual student. Who would benefit from private sessions?

- Those who have specific issues such as shoulder or back problems

- Students who are having trouble with a particular asana, want to develop a home practice, or deepen into some aspect of yoga

- Individuals who are uncomfortable coming into a large class to start

- People who simply want one-on-one attention

Do your students know that you offer private sessions? Do you have a flyer or brochure promoting this? Is it on your web site? Private sessions can average anywhere from $75 to $125 or more per class. What if you added just one private class a week to your teaching schedule? That could easily mean $5000 plus a year in additional revenue. What if you added several per week? If you own a studio with many teachers offering private sessions you can enjoy additional revenue for either space rental or a commission from your teachers.

Another type of specialized class that can be very successful is *introductory series*.

You need to regularly bring new students into your classes and introductory classes are a great way to do this. Additionally they can be very profitable.

Many potential students are scared to join an ongoing yoga class. They think that they might not perform well enough, are shy, have an injury, or are not flexible enough. Of course we know that none of these are "real" reasons not to come to class so the introductory class makes it very easy for these people to try yoga. We've seen 4 week series work very well with introductions.

RETREATS AND YOGA VACATIONS

Yoga retreats have become quite popular. Retreats give students an opportunity to deepen into their practice of yoga while enjoying the benefit of traveling to someplace beautiful and desirable, such as: Hawaii, Sedona, Mexico, Costa Rica, Europe, etc. They usually combine intensive yoga practice with plenty of down time to enjoy the venue. Retreats can be for a day, weekend, a week, or longer. They can be quite profitable and students who attend love them! We recommend that you start marketing retreats 6 months out from the date of your event. This will give you plenty of time to market and fill your event.

When selecting a retreat facility be sure to do a profit and loss analysis first. How much will it cost you to bring each student? How many students do you need to break even? How much profit will you make per student? What is the maximum number of students you can bring? What is the minimum? How long will your retreat be? How much will marketing cost?

If you have a large studio, it is very possible to run 2-3 retreats a year with each netting $10,000 or more. Even if you are teacher with a small following and run one retreat it can easily net you thousands of dollars.

TEACHER TRAININGS

Once you have developed following of dedicated yoga practitioners it is time to consider offering a yoga teacher training. This can have three significant benefits: First, it is a great opportunity for students who want to go deeper into their practice. Second, you will have a pool of yoga teachers to draw from when students finish the program. And finally, you will have an opportunity to gain significant profits.

> *If you have 20 students in a program that has a fee of $5,000 per student – that is $80,000 in revenue!*

The fee for an average teacher training program can range anywhere from $2,500 to $7,500 per student. If you have 20 students in a program that has a fee of $5,000 per student – that is $80,000 in revenue! Be sure to have highly experienced teachers running these programs – if you don't have them on staff, you'll want to bring them in from the outside.

INCREASING THE FREQUENCY OF STUDENT CLASS VISITS

When you look at how often your students attend your classes you probably notice a variety of themes:

- Those who attend 3 or more times per week.

- Those who attend 2 times per week.

- Those who attend 1 time a week.

- Those who attend once in a while.

What would happen if each of the students who were attending 1-2 times per week started attending just one more time per week? And what would happen if you could get some of the people who are not attending regularly to attend more often. What impact would these changes have on your bottom line? Depending on how you structure your class fees it could be significant! You could see additional income from class fees, more ancillary purchases for products and services, and additional referrals. Your students would also be gaining more of the benefits yoga has to offer which will get them more committed to the practice. As we all know, practicing just once a week is not enough!

Let's look at some ways to build class size and loyalty.

- *Your expertise:* Your students practice with you because of your expertise. They look to you as a yoga expert and professional. As such, we believe it is the teacher's responsibility to indicate to students how often they should practice. How often do students ask you the question: "How many time a week should I practice?" This is a common question, but for every person who asks there are 3 or 4 that don't even know to ask the question.

  Let's say you have someone who has back problems coming to your class once a week and they are seeing some benefits. You know that they would greatly benefit from coming 2-3 times a week. Then why not tell them. You would be surprised how they will respond positively to your recommendation. We can say the same for someone who has shoulder issues, or is highly inflexible, or has anxiety, wants to lose weight, or has one of the many conditions that yoga can really help. It is our job as teachers to recommend to students how yoga should be used.

- *Reach out:* When students stop coming to class or they come sporadically, a simple phone call or email may be all that is needed to get them back to class. You might also find out more about what is going in their lives that has prevented them from coming to class. The student might also offer you some important feedback about your classes or studio that you need to know. In any case they will most likely be impressed that you took the time to reach to them, it shows you care.

- *Class offerings:* Are the classes you offer meeting the needs of your students and studio for the long term? Do you have a lot of beginning level classes but no plans for intermediate and advanced classes? Conversely, are you offering a lot of intermediate and beginning level classes but don't have any way of bringing new students into your classes? Both of these scenarios could be a recipe for attrition (drop out). Remember, it is always more costly and time consuming to bring new students in than it is to cultivate the relationships you have with current ones.

  You will also find that some students always want the same thing, others want classes that are new and different and some students want a combination of these two. What are you doing to meet the needs of these groups?

  As mentioned earlier a good way to find out what kinds of classes students want is simply to ask them. You can do this informally, with a written questionnaire, or online. You can also get a good idea of what kind of classes are in demand by visiting other yoga studios both in your area and out of your area.

- *Referrals:* Referral programs are a very effective method for bringing new students to your classes AND they also can be an excellent way of motivating existing students to come to class. Many people like to practice with their friends and doing so helps motivate each other to get to class.

Some simple ways to implement a referral program include handing out referral cards, inserting them into newsletters, and doing special promotions. We have presented many ideas for these promotional methods early in the book.

- *Packaging classes:* There are many way to package and price your class offerings. How you do this has such a significant impact on your bottom line and the success of your studio that we have dedicated a significant portion of the next chapter to this discussion.

For now though, recognize that you can and should package classes to build loyalty, retention and give strong incentives for people to attend classes more often and/or for a longer period of time.

A fairly common practice is to package classes by number purchased such as a 10 class-card or 20 class-card. You can also simply charge by the time frame and/or number of times per week.

While we know that you most likely will have to accommodate the occasional drop-in student, we recommend pricing these classes much higher to discourage widespread use of drop-in classes and get people committed to their programs whenever possible.

By packaging classes, students will be more committed to their practice, you will get class fees up front, and you will have taken an important step in eliminating the ups and down of cash flow problems which affect many teachers and studios.

CHAPTER 10

SALES - HOW TO DIFFERENTIATE YOURSELF FROM COMPETITORS

"SELL." For many people in the yoga business this is considered a four letter word! In fact, the whole topic of selling is such a touchy one in this industry that we decided to wait till this very late chapter to broach the subject. NOT because we think sales aren't important, but rather quite the opposite. The process of selling is so important that we wanted to first get you engaged, thinking about marketing and earning your trust before we started talking about sales.

Whether you like it or not, sales is a critical part of any business' success if you are selling a product or service to the public. Think about it: money doesn't change hands until a sale is made. Why, then, do some people have such a negative association towards sales? Perhaps they had a really bad personal experience at a car dealership or a health club? Maybe their spiritual beliefs to serve human kind have them conflicted with the thought of taking other people's money—even when they are providing a valuable service in return. There could be any number of reasons but the reality is that if you want to succeed in your business long-term you will have to embrace selling.

> " ...selling is nothing more than educating an individual on making the best decision possible.

What is ironic is that if you have ever been the recipient of a good sales process you understand that selling is nothing more than educating an individual on making the best decision possible. Certainly there are skills and strategies that are designed to increase a salesperson's success in motivating the person to buy BUT no salesperson ever removes the wallet from your pocket and takes the money out! Ultimately it is the consumer who makes the buying decision; it is the salesperson's job to engage and educate you on the value of their product or service with the hopes that you will buy.

Selling simply means being a good communicator: you ask questions, you listen and you share the benefits of your services and products. If you learn how to do this properly you will never have to push anyone into buying something from you. Rather, you will actually motivate them to want to buy.

There are entire books written on the process of selling and the various skills and techniques that can be used in a presentation. If you feel you need some help with your sales skills then we suggest you get a book or attend a training course. The co-author of this book, Casey, has one of the most popular books on sales in the health and fitness industry entitled "Selling Fitness; the complete guide to selling health club memberships." Although it is specifically geared towards the selling of a fitness membership the process can be easily applied to selling yoga. For more information you can visit www.HealthClubSalesTraining.com. In this book let's simply outline the basic sales process. Once done, we can turn our focus on the strategy of selling for yoga studios, identify the biggest challenges you will face, and provide you with some solutions.

THE SALES PROCESS

There are 8 steps to the selling process. Before we discuss each one in greater detail, here is an outline of the steps.

1. Get a prospect

2. Meet & Greet/Pre-qualify

3. Needs Analysis/Qualify

4. Educate/Present product options

5. Discuss pricing

6. Answer questions/Address objections

7. Encourage referrals

8. Follow up

If you are new to the sales process, we recommend that you implement one step a week for eight weeks. In this way you will learn the sales process without being overwhelmed. On the other hand you may already be doing some of these things and the information below will help to refine your sales process and make it more successful.

GET A PROSPECT

Obviously nothing can be sold unless you are talking to a potential customer. The first half of this book focused almost entirely on the marketing process—i.e. how to spend your time and money generating prospects. The primary difference as it relates to the sales process is simply scope. Where marketing is something that a company does to try and reach large amounts of people, prospecting as discussed in the context of sales process is more about individual outreach. As an individual, what can I do on a daily basis to find prospects?

Certainly as the owner-operator of your business this seems like a very obvious and logical thing to do. Unfortunately, many business owners let prospecting opportunities pass them by every day. Do you give your business card to the girl at the coffee shop that you stop by every morning? Do you leave a class pass or business card behind every time you are at a restaurant and leave your money or credit card receipt in the folio? When you are at the supermarket and someone says something about your branded yoga jacket or shirt do you encourage them to give you their contact details so you can send them a free pass through an e-mail link? Of course, these are just a few of the dozens of daily interactions you might have. The question you need to ask yourself is, "Am I making the most out of every interaction I have to locate and/or generate potential prospects?"

We are not suggesting that you are pushy or obnoxious about it! But to use a famous analogy, "You can't hit the ball if you don't step up to the plate." So what if the person says "No, not interested in yoga," or you watch them throw your card away after you turn to walk away. Sales is a numbers game and "The more contacts you make, the more sales you make." The bottom line is, that in addition to your larger marketing efforts look for opportunities to prospect each and every day.

MEET & GREET/PRE-QUALIFY

The meet and greet refers to the first one-on-one interaction that you have with a prospect. There may be times when you speak to a prospect over the phone before they come in to visit or attend a class. This means that you would have some connection with them before your first meeting but the first face-to-face is important. First impressions can't be re-made.

Because those of you reading this book represent a diverse set of business circumstances there are many possibilities for how a meet and greet might happen. If you own a studio maybe you have a small front desk or lobby area that the new student walks into first. Depending upon the size it may or may not have a front desk attendant. If your studio is attached to your home or you rent space from a recreational center there may not be any type of "greeting" area. We can't identify every single situation here but suffice it to say that some basic elements to a meet and greet are essential.

First, do you have a process for identifying guests or first time visitors/students? Often times this is easy because the person is looking around and trying to figure out what to do and where to go. Do you make it easier for them with signage that clearly directs guests or first time users what to do so they don't have to feel or look like the "newbie?" Are you warmly greeting each person with a welcoming smile, introducing yourself and asking them for their name? Are you literally saying to them, "Welcome, I'm glad you visited us today?" Sounds so simple but if you visit as many yoga studios as we do you would be shocked at the greetings we get (or don't).

> *...make it easier for them with signage that clearly directs guests or first time users what to do...*

Another aspect to the meet and greet is called the pre-qualifying. Pre-qualifying refers to a process by which you initially identify the type of prospect that is standing in front of you and what it is they want from their visit. This way you can be sure to provide them with exactly the information they want. Some of the key pieces of information you would want to obtain from your guests would include the following: Are they here to take a class? (Probably, but don't assume.) Have they ever been to one of your classes before? (This question can be appropriate for "your class" as an individual or "your classes" as a studio. Hopefully if it is the former you will at least recognize the person.) How did they hear about you? (This is really important for your marketing statistics.) Do they live local or are they just visiting? Have they ever taken a yoga class before? Do they have any medical restrictions you should know of? And, if they are going to take a class, ask them if they have all the items they will need—mat, towel, water, strap, etc.

NEEDS ANALYSIS/QUALIFY

Once you have gotten through a basic pre-qualifying and understand whether or not the person in front of you is a potential on-going student, it's nice if you can get some additional personal information from them. In selling this is called the qualifying process but we prefer to call it the "Needs Analysis." Specifically, your goal is to better understand the needs and wants of this person as it relates to participating in your yoga classes so you can help them make a buying decision.

At this point some of you may be thinking, "What do you mean make a buying decision; the person is there to take a class and either has a free pass, a discount coupon or is expecting to hand you some money. Haven't they already made a buying decision?" Our answer to that is, "No; they have made an 'I'll give it a try' decision!" By taking some time and getting to know this person better you will establish a greater level of rapport. It is relationships that keep people coming back, not just great yoga classes (those are pre-requisites).

Your ability to take time to do a Needs Analysis with someone will depend upon the situation. Obviously, if this person came in 4 minutes before your class begins this type of deeper conversation isn't going to happen right then. In that instance you will be lucky to get through the basic pre-qualifying questions and get them onto their mat without being late. So, you must recognize that doing a Needs Analysis might happen over the phone when someone calls in for information; it might be that the person stops by when no class is happening and you have time to chat, or it might happen after a class. Heck, it might not happen at all for a variety of reasons but in a perfect world it is best to try and spend some time with prospects to better understand them, their exercise history, their goals and motivation for starting yoga or leaving another studio to try yours.

There are three categories of questions that are relevant to your conversation with a prospect during the Needs Analysis. First is their exercise history. Second is their goals and motivation. Third is discovering if there are any potential roadblocks that may get in their way from starting or sticking with the classes.

With exercise history we aren't referring to the basic question of whether or not they have done yoga before. Remember that you already asked that during the meet and greet. Here we are referring to the details of what type of yoga they have done, where was did they take class, how often did they participate, and when was their last class? If they have never done yoga before it is still good to ask them about their exercise history. What type of exercise do they participate in and how often? If they aren't currently exercising when was the last time they were? This type of information is important for you to know so you can help guide them during the class as well as provide them with an expectation before participating.

The next aspect of the Needs Analysis is understanding the persons' goals and motivation. If someone is new, why do they want to do yoga? This is important because if you want students to be happy, long-term participants you need to ensure they are getting what they want from their practice. Do they want to gain flexibility, lose weight, recover from an injury or maybe they simply are looking for a new, low impact form of exercise? Everyone will be different. For a current practitioner, why are they coming to check out your class? What specifically are they looking for that they are not getting from their current practice, whether it is at home or at another location? Obviously you aren't going to change your classes based on the students but if you understand what a student wants and why that is important to them you might be able to adjust certain poses or provide them with particular education or motivation that will make them as happy as possible.

The last part of a complete Needs Analysis is uncovering any potential roadblocks or challenges that this person may have with their practice. There are basic logistical things like "Do we have classes at times that meet their scheduling needs," and "Are we conveniently located" but there are other, more personal and subtle roadblocks that could hinder whether someone starts and sticks with your classes. If they are new, what is their comfort level with the learning curve? Would it be advantageous for them to have an exercise partner because they are prone to dropping out? Are there any issues with their travel or lifestyle that might result in an inconsistent practice? By knowing these things you are in a good position to help them to work through such obstacles.

For someone who has no formal sales training the Needs Analysis can initially seem overwhelming. Many instructors will ask us, "Do I really need to ask the prospect all those personal questions when they are just coming in for a class?" Well, no, you don't *need* to do any of these things but doing so will result in a stronger relationship with the individual. What we know is that people prefer to buy from people they like! When you show an interest in others they feel important and as the instructor or studio owner it shows that you sincerely care and want them to get the most from their yoga practice.

EDUCATE/PRESENT PRODUCT OPTIONS

Once you have a solid understanding of a person's yoga or exercise history, goals and motivation, and potential roadblocks or obstacles you can then discuss with them how your classes and/or studio fits what they are looking for. (In some cases you may have to tell them you don't have what they are looking for.) This is typically the easiest part of the sales process for most yoga instructors because they are confident in talking about their classes and they are passionate about discussing yoga! Although this is a good thing there is one caution; beware of the Disney presentation. Let's explain.

> ❝ ...a Disney presentation is when the salesperson continues to talk about their product or service without ever checking in with the prospect...

In sales a Disney presentation is when the salesperson continues to talk about their product or service without ever checking in with the prospect to get feedback. The analogy is that, like sitting on a tour bus in Disney, the prospect just listens to you blab on and on and then gets off the bus. The driver (you) has gotten no feedback as to whether or not the person found the information interesting or if what they saw was what they were looking for.

How you can prevent yourself from giving a Disney presentation is to condition yourself to ask the prospect for feedback after every few items of information. "Is that the type of yoga class that you were looking for?" "Is our schedule going to be conducive to yours?" and "Are we convenient to either your home or work place?" would be simple examples of how you would engage a prospect while educating them on what you offer.

DISCUSS PRICING

For many of you discussing price is simple because you charge a per class fee, end of subject. For others who may have class packs or specific programs, it is at this stage in the sales process that you typically discuss pricing with the prospect. The reason that you wait until this point is because you want to make sure a) you actually have what this person is looking for and b) that the prospect fully understands the value of your class and or studio.

ANSWER QUESTIONS/ ADDRESS OBJECTIONS

After you discuss the price, the prospect may have some questions or concerns. In sales if the customer gives you a reason why they don't want to buy this is called an objection. Yoga is not the type of product that gets a lot of objections so we aren't going to spend much time on the topic here. We do, however, want to make one important distinction. Know the difference between a condition and an objection.

A condition is something that is totally out of your control. You don't have classes at the time they have available; the studio isn't convenient for them, or; the person was looking for one type of yoga and you don't teach that style. There is nothing that you can do to change these things, hence why these are called conditions.

An objection, on the other hand, is a perception by the prospect as to why they may not want to become a student of yours. The person has never done yoga before and they are concerned they won't be able to get the hang of it without feeling embarrassed, or; they want to exercise 3 times per week but when they do the math it will be out of their budget so they don't want to take any classes. The difference with objections is that you have the ability to influence that person's perception of the situation based upon what you say to them.

The goal with objections, of course, is to try and uncover them during the Needs Analysis and then use the educational stage of the sales process to help change the person's perception. For example, if you identified that they wanted to come in three times per week but they also told you they were only working part time at the moment, it would be good to educate them on the benefits of yoga even once a week.

NOTE: At this point in the discussion it is important to note that although we have these broken down into stages, the steps of the sales process often happen at light speed with the meet & greet, qualifying, educating and discussing options and pricing options all happening almost simultaneously. This is normal and we break it down for training purposes so you can understand each component fully. In addition, sometimes this process happens over the phone, sometimes it's before a class and sometimes afterwards. It's all good so long as you are trying to obtain the information, gain rapport and have some fun in the process.

ENCOURAGE REFERRALS

The next step in the sales process is probably the most underutilized in the yoga industry; encouraging the new student to bring friends. What is ironic is that most yoga classes gain popularity because students brag to their friends. So, referrals are happening organically all the time. However, many instructors can be uncomfortable with requesting referrals. We are not suggesting that you ask them for the phone numbers of their friends so you can call them. What we are suggesting is that you have some kind of referral program in place where a new student is given an incentive to refer other new members.

FOLLOW UP

The final step in the sales process is follow-up. This means two things. First, if the student takes a class but doesn't show up for a week, reach out to them and try and obtain valuable information. How did they like the class? Were they planning on coming back again? Did they know about an upcoming special class? Remember that for most yoga classes and studios there is no membership model whereby the person is paying a flat monthly fee whether they show up or not. If someone came in and took a class but hasn't come back in a week or two, it is in your best interest to try and discover why. More importantly was there anything that you could have done differently that would have changed the outcome?

> *The final step in the sales process is follow-up.*

"SELLING YOGA"; IS IT AN OXYMORON?

As we discussed very early in this book, it is not uncommon for yoga instructors to be uncomfortable with the sales process. Yogis don't want to come across as pushy and often believe that an individual can make up their own mind without any undue influence from others. We agree that there is no place for pushy sales tactics in selling yoga (or anything for that matter). There is, however, the need to clearly educate and motivate individuals; particularly those that are new to yoga.

> *You need to ask people to take action.*

Spending time to learn about a prospects exercise history, needs, and wants is going to help you to customize how you educate and motivate potential students. Even with all that, one thing is missing. You need to ask people to take action. "Did you like the class enough to come back?" "Would you like to sign up for one of our 12-week packages?" Or, "Is the studio meeting your expectations?" are three simple examples of asking someone to take action.

As you can see "asking" isn't just about saying, cash, check or credit card! Asking is the entire process of checking in with a prospect in a way that identifies whether or not they like what they are experiencing and encouraging them to continue if you get a positive response. What you don't want to do is ask them nothing—or questions that don't tell you anything about their buying decision—and then wonder why they never came back. We're not saying that this will come naturally to all of you, but it is a skill that will develop over time—especially if you want the best possible chances for your business to succeed.

TECHNOLOGY IN SALES

The good news is that for those of you who are uncomfortable with selling, technology does help assist in the process. Back in chapter 5 we discussed how to choose an autoresponder system. Although we were talking about the marketing process, an autoresponder system can be utilized after a prospect has taken a class. It is simple to set up a series of educational, follow up messages that help to emphasize the benefits of both yoga and your classes or studio. Best of all, you can set up the timing of the sequence to keep the person motivated by encouraging them to get back in.

At the end of the day the best approach is a combination of both. Fantastic rapport and personal skills to engage a prospect when they visit your class or enquire combined with a safety net of autoresponders that make the person feel as though you care about them and want to earn their business. And, really, that is what selling is all about. You provide people with the absolute best product and service so they want to buy from you! Once you have earned their business then you need to earn their continued business. So, let's turn now to the topic of retention.

CHAPTER 11

THE SECRETS FOR DEVELOPING LONG-TERM STUDENTS

At this point, no doubt you appreciate the incredible financial impact that one customer can have on your bottom line. By keeping students coming regularly to class (and hopefully increasing their usage), you can dramatically increase the amount of revenue your business generates. Even better, you can create a raving fan at the same time!

The question every business struggles with is, "How to keep customers coming?" In the fitness industry this topic is referred to as retention. Believe it or not, retention is really just as important as sales. Think about it; if you are losing new customers as fast as you obtain them it would be the equivalent of treading water—financially. You want to build your business so you are constantly improving revenue.

> " *...it is less expensive to keep a customer happy than it is to generate a new customer.*

Most businesses don't realize that it is less expensive to keep a customer happy than it is to generate a new customer. Unfortunately, it is human nature to lose sight of this and not put as much energy and effort into keeping current customers happy. The good news, however, is that there are lots of little things you can do with your studio and practice that will cause students to have exceptional experiences with you and keep them attending class and referring others.

In Chapter 7 we presented a number of ideas for increasing sales and meeting the needs of your students through class offerings, services and products. Both of these areas directly impact your bottom line. In this chapter we address the elements that directly affect customer experience and influence building long-term relationships with them.

WHAT IS "GOOD CUSTOMER SERVICE?"

Get a group of business owners in a room and ask them to define "good customer service" and you will have as many opinions as you have individuals. In fact, it's probably easier to define what good customer service isn't.

We have all been in situations where we walked into a store and the clerk remained on their cell phone without even a hint of looking up while we impatiently waited for them to either hang up or make eye contact. Or perhaps it was the time you were at a restaurant and the waiter wasn't attentive to your needs. Maybe it was something as simple as asking a store employee where something was located and instead of walking you there, they pointed in the general direction and said, "Over that way." These may sound like extreme examples but the sad reality is that we are subjected to horrible customer service each and every day. So much so that when we get exceptional customer service we are shocked. Delighted but shocked.

THE 10:1 RULE

If you have taken any customer service trainings you may be familiar with the 10:1 rule. It states that it takes ten positive customer service experiences before an individual becomes confident that your business has its act together. Sadly, it only takes one negative experience for consumer confidence to become eroded! For those of us who own a business that can be a depressing thought, but it really hits home the importance of ensuring that every interaction a customer has is a positive one. This logically makes sense and yet can be challenging to maintain.

Small businesses owners have a tremendous amount of multitasking to do. Most yoga studio owners are the chief cook and bottle washer of their facility—at least in the early days. Of course, yoga instructors growing their individual practices are in charge of every aspect of their business. The challenge with this is, that it becomes difficult to pay attention to all the little details. Furthermore, some people have personalities that are more attuned to details while others are big picture. These personality types approach customer service differently. The key is taking a "personal inventory" of your customer service skills and attitude and finding ways to improve the experience that your students will receive.

Like the subject of sales, there are entire books and courses dedicated to providing exceptional customer service. For our purposes let's specifically outline the aspects of customer service that are particular to the yoga studio world. These are not in any particular order and all are important to consider.

CLASS SCHEDULE TIMES

It sounds like the obvious but we are amazed at the number of studios or teachers that establish classes based on what is best for their teaching schedule and not the students' schedule. This is a big mistake since you are trying to make it easy for your students to attend. Choosing class times that are before and after work make sense. For moms you need a time that is after buses but before the half day pick up mark. Make sure you do some research on the school schedules in your area before you finalize any class times.

The number of classes you offer is also important. This applies more to studios and full time instructors and it can be a tough balance to find in the early days of your business. Obviously the more classes you offer the more chances you have of attracting a diverse population of students. However, if you offer too many classes too early, you actually dilute the number of students per class. This results in a low profitability per class. As a result we suggest that you start with enough classes to cover the prime times but only add classes as these become full.

COMMUNICATION

Have you ever showed up for a yoga class and there was a sign on the door saying that the hours have changed or that "Due to illness there will be no class tonight"? No matter how understanding you may be, this type of situation is one of those experiences that erode confidence in a business.

> *Communication with your students is a critical aspect of your customer service.*

Communication with your students is a critical aspect of your customer service. Are there any changes in class times or instructors? Are you adding or removing certain classes? Will there be a substitute teacher because you are away for vacation? Is the studio going to be closed for one day to have the floors re-finished? Is there some kind of special seminar that is happening and space is limited?

This is where technology, building your e-mail lists and using a contact management system pays off. Imagine that you have your students categorized in your data base by the specific class they attend. If there is going to be a change to that class, you would be able to send out an e-mail broadcast with the push of one button! No need to send out information to the entire student list or individually send emails. Technology allows for targeted, effective communication. Of course, there may be times when it is appropriate to send out information to the entire student body and post it on your Facebook page. The beauty is that when you have all these things set up you can do such things quickly and easily.

By keeping your students informed about all that is happening, you show you care about them and are going the extra mile to make sure they are in the know.

CLEANLINESS

As speakers and authors, we both have the good fortune of travelling for work and visiting lots of studios. There is nothing more disturbing than putting your yoga mat down on the studio floor and watching dust bunnies fly all around! You might be laughing, but we are amazed at the number of studios that don't pay close enough attention to the cleanliness of their facilities. Again, this is another one of those things that if you are "doing it all," it is easy to let slack. But knowing that most yoga students are women— and one of the most important things to women in public places is cleanliness—this is an area of customer service that you must be highly attentive to. Here is a list of common areas to watch:

- Be certain that the hard wood floors are dry mopped after each class to ensure no dust or hair is floating around.

- Vacuum before each class so the rugs are totally clean— especially the corners and cove bases.

- Check the lobby/entrance area to make sure it is clean and neat. If people have left things behind put them into a lost and found box. If you have a table for brochures or class schedules make sure it is organized.

- Mats, blocks and other props! If you have "public" items (whether free or for a small charge), are you making sure these are sanitized? Do you roll up the straps or at least have them in a basket so they aren't just thrown in a corner getting tangled? Same for blankets. Are they washed regularly and folded neatly when put away after classes?

- Bathrooms. This is a huge pet peeve for many women! Aside from the obvious cleanliness issue, does it have paper towels and toilet paper with extra on the shelf to ensure no one gets caught short? How about the soap; is it environmentally friendly?

- Exterior. If you own a studio, whether you actually own the space or are renting, is the outside inviting? Is the doorway clean of hand prints? Have you planted some flowers? What about seasonal decorations that make the environment more friendly and fun? The exterior is the first impression that a prospect will have of your business so make sure it is a good one.

CROWDEDNESS

One of the first things we discussed in this section was the number of class offerings. Obviously you need to manage your classes so that you have the right balance between students and profitability. One of the biggest complaints of students is that the class is too crowded. It's an interesting thing to monitor because where yoga is all about "staying on your own mat" and "seeing the light in the person next to you," if it gets too crowded all that goes out the window!

Every type of yoga has different guidelines for how crowded a class could and should be and obviously this is going to be a personal decision you make. What you want to do is be aware of how the students are feeling and be certain to stay within a comfort zone so as to not turn off too many.

INSTRUCTOR INTRODUCTION

Another customer service concept that might be the "blinding flash of the obvious" is introductions. We are amazed, however, at the number of classes we attend where the instructor starts class without a single bit of introduction. Sure, if you know all your students and it is a class that runs for 12-weeks you certainly don't need to introduce yourself every class but we are talking about drop-in formats.

> " We are amazed, however, at the number of classes we attend where the instructor starts class without a single bit of introduction.

When possible, get to the class early and say hello to students using their name. People love to be recognized. Are you welcoming the students and pre-framing them "We are going to have an awesome class tonight" or "Tonight we are going to be working on headstands," something like that. Give them friendly reminders that they should stay within their own comfort level, not do anything that hurts, and modify poses as needed.

NEW STUDENT INTEGRATION

We realize that most good yoga training programs cover how to intergrate new students into an ongoing class. Because a student's first time experience is so important we are reviewing a few key points on how to do that here.

- If a student new to yoga is going to be placed into a mainstream class, be sure to put them in a location where they can see students on all sides of their mat while being mindful that they don't feel like they are on display. Just as importantly, you want to be able to see them so you can help them as necessary. All too often new students want to "hide" in the back of the class – the last place they should be.

- Explain to the new student why you are placing them where you are AND that there is no right or wrong with a yoga class. Every "body" is different and the only thing they need to worry about is taking care of themself. This sounds so cliché but is what they need to hear.

- If possible, introduce the new student to one or two of the students around them. This should be done quietly so that the new student doesn't feel like "the new kid" in the class.

- During class be mindful of not correcting the new person in a way that makes them feel like they are being isolated out. Certainly make sure that they aren't hurting themselves but try not to overly correct them. What is important is that they are there.

- After class check in with the new student. Compliment them on how well they did—even if they were disastrous. Try and encourage them to get to the next class soon.

IT'S THE LITTLE THINGS

We've all heard the express that "It's the little things that make a difference." So, what does that mean when it comes to customer service at your studio or in your classes? There could be a lot of things but some of the small things that we hear make a difference include:

- Is the studio well decorated in a tasteful way that instills a yogic environment? We realize that instructors renting don't always have total control over this but could you bring props or portable items that help?

- Do you have mats available for new students to borrow? If you are going to charge for them, do you make those available at a reasonable fee?

- Do you provide tissues in the class? It sounds so simple but is very frustrating to students when the box is out.

- If you run a studio do you make basic toiletries available for emergency situations? Having tampons, hair bands, safety pins and other small items available with a sign asking people to use only when necessary is a nice touch.

SERVICE PHILOSOPHY

Recently while doing a marketing audit for a client we analyzed all the student reviews and suggestions. One theme that continued to show up was "Being nickel & dimed." The expression refers to a business that charges customers for every single little thing. Of course, we are in business to make a profit and you can't provide things if they cost you more than their return. But you have to weigh certain things and ask yourself, "Is this really costing me anything in the long run?"

Case in point is yoga mats for visiting students. A lot of facilities will charge students $2 to rent a yoga mat. Yoga mats do cost money and they will eventually need to be replaced but is collecting $2 from a first time visitor who is already paying a $15 fee for class necessary? Will it leave the impression that you are trying to squeeze out every single penny from that person? Would it be better to buy a bulk roll of yoga mat material and make ten mats that have the business name written on them and are made available for visiting students and those that might have forgotten their mat? We don't know the answer for you, but our experience is that studios who charge for mat use (no matter the situation), charge $2.50 for a .50 bottle of water and are asking $18 per class have more student comments that question the business' philosophy.

What we are suggesting here is that you find a balance between your profit centers and small customer service items that have a positive impact without a lot of expense to you.

> *...find a balance between your profit centers and small customer service items...*

BIRTHDAY CARDS

Have you ever gotten a birthday card from someone you have done business with? Perhaps it was a salesman from whom you bought a car or your investment broker? Maybe they even sent you a little gift like a small box of chocolates? Even if you didn't like the gift you probably thought to yourself, "Wow, that was really nice." This is especially true if the card is purely sent to wish you a Happy Birthday and doesn't include some kind of promotion on their part.

It would not be difficult to ask new students for their birthdate during the enrollment process and then send them a card. Better yet, why not send them a card that has a coupon in it for a free class. Starbucks does this quite well. When you enroll in their frequent buyer program they send you an e-mail message that says "The next one is on us" and they load your card with a free drink. Although electronic, and in our opinion not as impactful as a real card sent through the mail, this is a brilliant strategy. Here we are, writing to thousands of people about this—bragging about the customer service. This is exactly why companies like Starbucks do these types of things; they make a positive experience for the customer that helps to create a stronger bond with their brand.

You can buy blank Avery cards from your local office supply store and create your own, inexpensive birthday cards. Use the Avery business card sheets and you can even create the free class coupons. Of course, you can do this through such services like GotPrint and VistaPrint to ensure the highest quality printing. These companies will even help you over the phone with basic layout and graphics.

USAGE GAMES

In the previous chapter discussing how to increase the frequency of students' visits we outlined a number of programs you could implement. All of those things should also have a positive impact on retention. You can go one step farther with these types of ideas and run games where there is a bit more fun integrated into the concept. This is a very popular happening in the fitness industry and only takes a small amount of creativity to apply it to your yoga studio or classes.

One example is the Olympics. Many fitness facilities will run a competition during the Olympics whereby members complete a variety of different classes and activities in a given period of time and they receive a T-shirt or an entry into a raffle for a larger prize. During the Tour de France, clubs will put a map of the bike route onto the wall. Every exercise session is equivalent to a certain number of miles on the route. When the member crosses the finish line within a time period there is an incentive or reward.

Many yoga instructors argue that this type of activity is appropriate for fitness centers but not for yoga because the students don't have the same competitiveness or philosophy on "exercise." That could absolutely be true for your type of classes and this certainly isn't for everyone. But before you make a judgment perhaps a better question would be, "How can I find a way to incorporate usage programs into my classes that would appeal to my students?" Whether an individual is taking yoga, going to the gym or participating in tai chi classes, human nature tells us that people like to have fun and like to work towards goals and incentives.

Here are few ideas to get you started:

- Yoga Boot Camp

- Eight Weeks of Inversions

- Summer yoga challenge (could be any time of year)

Reward students for showing up twice a week for 3 months. Rewards can be at different levels and you can offer anything from free T-shirts, to free classes, to books or DVDs, etc.

CONNECTIONS

One of the most powerful influences of retention is the relationships that your students form with both the instructors and the other students. There is absolutely something to the power of the Cheers television program jingle, "Where everybody knows your name." When you walk into yoga class and people say, "Hey, Casey, where have you been?" Or the instructor works their way through the class saying hello to everyone <u>and</u> uses their names, it is powerful and it has a profound, unconscious effect on how someone feels about participating.

> One of the most powerful influences of retention is the relationships that your students form...

In the book *Pour Your Heart Into It* by Howard Schultz, founder of Starbucks, he talks about how the company's goal was to have Starbucks become the third place in someone's life. Home, work and Starbucks! One of the ways in which the company does this is by using your name in the ordering process. The cashier asks you for your name and writes it on the cup. When the Barista is done he or she calls out your name along with the drink you have ordered. "I have a tall, skinny, caramel macchiato for Howard." Three important things happen when this is done. First, you are hearing your name multiple times. Everyone loves to hear their own name. Second, there is a form of social proof in hearing your drink along with your name. It reinforces that "this is my choice for a drink" and makes you take ownership. Finally, the store gets to know your name and they use it the next time you come into the store. This creates that Cheers-like environment.

Having that strong, connective environment inside the studio will certainly help with retention but if you want to take it to an even deeper level then what you need to do is create what Seth Godin refers to as a tribe.

In his book *Tribes,* Godin talks extensively about the power of connections among people and how creating the feeling of a tribe amongst customers is highly influential in any businesses success. In a way, that is exactly what you are trying to do with your studio—create a tribe of yoga students that want to stick together. One way to do this is to foster relationships outside of class times. Seminars, workshops and retreats will certainly aid in this but there are other things you can do to foster this as well. Organize going out to cultural events together. We know one studio that takes quarterly outings to new-age musical performances. Another studio organizes weekend hikes for people with dogs. Heck, even if it was informally getting together for dinner and a movie there will be plenty of people who are looking for more of a social connection. We have also heard of yoga students creating book clubs, meditation groups, theater groups, etc. Community is so important, why not encourage this!

One word of advice is to be consistent in your early efforts. Often it will take time for people to fit new activities into their schedule and/or hear about the event enough times to give it a try. By creating these relationships outside of classes you will create much deeper connections amongst the students and keep them coming for longer.

CHAPTER 12
PLAYING BY THE NUMBERS

In the very first chapter of this book we discussed that the two critical factors in a business' financial success were cash flow and profitability. We recognize that you didn't get into the yoga business only for financial success but, as we have stated before, if you aren't financially successful you won't be able to keep teaching classes. Although those are the two most fundamental numbers that determine whether or not you keep your doors open, there are other numbers that are important to monitor. In fact, only by monitoring certain Key Performance Indicators (KPI's) will you be able to improve your business.

BUT NUMBERS AREN'T THAT IMPORTANT TO ME!

We know that some of you are saying that to yourself right now. Okay, if numbers aren't that important to you in business then by all means please put this book down now and get to work on all the other things we have discussed. But for those of you who want to maximize your level of success and your profits then please continue to read on.

"What gets measured gets improved."

Whether it is an Olympic athlete, a school report card or a profit and loss statement, measurement allows us to see progress or decline. We hope by now you have realized that there are many things that will influence the bottom line of your business. In fact, measuring the actual profitability and cash flow is rather simple. It is measuring all the things that will influence those numbers that becomes more challenging; not because it is difficult but because it takes time and discipline.

> " *...measurement allows us to see progress or decline.*

Aside from measuring improvement, another benefit of tracking your KPI's is identifying trends. It may be obvious that you get the largest influx of new students in January. You probably don't even need to measure that to know, BUT what if you could identify the exact month (maybe even week) where the biggest drop off in usage occurred after the influx? With that information you could establish a usage game or program that might keep more students coming. We have all heard the expression, "You can't see the forest through the trees." With trends you are able to step back and see the bigger picture of your KPI's giving you valuable insights into your business' performance.

YOUR KPI'S

There are many KPI's that can be tracked, just ask your accountant. The more numbers you track, the more information you have regarding what is working and what isn't. Below we are going to list out the more important KPI's for a yoga business.

NUMBER OF ACTIVE STUDENTS

This number needs no explanation as we have dedicated an entire chapter to the first way to grow revenue—get more customers. Suffice it to say that you need to know how many active, paying students you have in any given month.

NET GAIN/LOSS OF STUDENTS PER MONTH

By tracking the number of active students each month you will know whether or not you are gaining more students or losing them. In business this figure is referred to as a net customer gain or loss. Because you know that more students should mean more revenue, you want to do everything possible—even through seasonal changes in attendance patterns—to try either gain students or at the very least maintain them.

AVERAGE PER CLASS REVENUE

There will come a time when you are super successful and your classes will be full. In any business, if you have reached capacity it typically means your prices are too low. You may be totally happy with the average cost of class and leave your prices where they are, but you may discover that because of a price discount you are "leaving money on the table." Again, you won't know until you track it.

To determine the average class cost you are simply going to take the total number of student visits for all classes that month and divide it into the total revenue collected on classes. To make the example easy, let's suppose you are teaching two classes per week for a total of eight classes in the month (some months it will be more because of the way the calendar falls). Some classes you had 9 students while others you had 21. In total you had 120 "student visits" (throughout the month). The total money you collected for the classes was $1,590. When you divide 120 into $1,590 you get an average of $13.25 per class. The odd amount was probably due to the fact that you offer discounted class packs. Some of the students purchased those while others paid the full drop in rate.

For those of you who are more interested in numbers you may be thinking, "Hey, I'd rather have a lower average class rate because that means more people are buying discounted packages, which means they are probably coming more frequently." The reply to that is, "You don't know that unless you are monitoring other numbers!" Other than profit, no one number can be seen as good or bad. You must look at a variety of KPI's and how they relate to one another. As daunting as this may seem to some, tracking your numbers will make you a much better business person.

AVERAGE PER-STUDENT VISITS

Again, we dedicated an entire section of this book to discussing how you can increase the frequency of each student's participation. To get this figure you take the total number of students actively visiting in one calendar month and divide that by the total number of class visits. Let's keep with our earlier example of having 120 "student visits" throughout the month. If that number represented a total of 32 individual students, you would divide 120 by 32 and get an average of 3.75. This would mean that the average number of classes each one of your students was taking per month was 3.75.

NUMBER OF STUDENTS
PER CLASS (ACTUAL)

Earlier we discussed the need to track the total number of "student visits" so that at the end of the month you can calculate the average per class revenue. Tracking the total number of students that attend each individual class has another benefit; it allows you to track which classes are getting the greatest attendance. For studio operators this is going to be very important for two reasons. One, to determine which instructors are the most popular and, two; what class times are the most well attended. This allows you to make the best instructor choices and scheduling modifications to best meet customer demand and profitability.

AVERAGE GROSS REVENUE PER STUDENT PER MONTH

Remember that our goal is to maximize the profitability of your business. Increasing the frequency of student visits and purchases obviously increases the overall gross revenue per student. To determine this figure you simply take the total number of active students you have in the month and divide it into the total revenue generated, including all ancillary income from retail sales.

Let's suppose that in addition to the $1590 you generated from class revenue last month you also had an additional $850 in sales from mats, T-shirts and book sales. This means your total revenue for the month would be $2,440. With 32 students your average per student revenue would be $76.25. If you were to calculate only ancillary revenue spend you would take the $850 and divide it by the 32, which would mean that the average student spent $26.56 on items other than classes in that calendar month.

AVERAGE NUMBER OF MONTHS A STUDENT STAYS ACTIVE

This next KPI is a very interesting one because it forces you to monitor the length in which a student remains active with your classes. Certainly you will have students who stay with you for years and years. Every yoga teacher has their "followers" but the reality is that human beings start and stop things all the time. This is particularly true when it comes to exercise participation. Furthermore, you will have people who move out of the area or for some reason or another move to another studio or instructor.

Obviously, the longer a student stays with you the better it is for business on many fronts. For sure it means consistent revenue. Perhaps even more important, however, is the potential for referrals. Students who stay with you are more likely to tell others about you and your classes. And you now know the power of referrals in relation to the growth of your business.

In monitoring this figure you must make a determination as to what constitutes an "inactive" student. If you live in a geographical area where students leave for a season this must be taken into consideration. As a general rule it is fair to say that if someone doesn't show up for three months in a row they could be considered inactive.

To determine this KPI it takes a software program that has advanced tracking capabilities because you need to be able to obtain the total number of months each student has been with you and divide that by the total number of active students.

Let's suppose that your software calculates the average time a student remains active is 6.5 months. Your next question is, "Is that good or bad?" Well, if you had only been in business for 8 months that would be a great statistic but it really doesn't mean anything unless you can compare it to something over the long-run. Ultimately what you want to see is students remaining active for years, not months. Over your years in business you will be able to see how the numbers are tracking and know whether your retention is getting better or worse.

LIFETIME VALUE OF A CUSTOMER

This next KPI is a favorite of marketing guru Jay Abraham. Lifetime value (LV) means exactly what it sounds like. What is the total value of revenue that one single customer will bring to your business. For new businesses this number is impossible to calculate. You won't be able to determine this number until customers begin to become inactive. Basically you will take the average number of active months for your students and multiply that by the average monthly revenue (both of these figures we calculated earlier.) The more months or years that you have figures tracked, the more accurate your calculations will become.

So, in our example the average number of months a student was staying was 6.5 and the average monthly revenue was $76.25. This would mean that the average LV of a student at this point in time of your business would be $495.62.

NOTE: When calculating the LV of a customer it is better to take yearly averages for the revenue when possible, because there are always fluctuations in income each month. This is particularly true for ancillary revenue. Therefore, to determine the average monthly income of a student you will want to take an average of all your individual month's calculations. So, perhaps in one month the revenue average was $76.25, a second month it was $101.55 and a third it was $94.56. Assuming you had only been open for these three months, the average for those months would be $90.78 in income per student. Now you would take that and multiple by the average number of months a student stays. It sounds complicated when you are reading it but this will become second nature to you once you begin to track the numbers.

AVERAGE PER SQUARE FOOT REVENUE

This is a KPI that many businesses don't track but it is one that is particularly interesting for yoga studios because it gives you an idea of how well you are maximizing your square footage. The number is quite easy to calculate; take the total square footage of your entire rented space and divide that into the total revenue for the month. This gives you the revenue per square foot. For anyone renting space, tracking this number makes you very focused on maximizing the usable square footage in your facility for either students or ancillary sales.

MARKETING KPI'S

Up to now all of the KPI's that we have discussed have to do with revenue. There is an entirely different set of KPI's relating to marketing (and another for sales). Let's discuss two of the most important marketing statistics.

Lead acquisition cost (LAC)

The first marketing KPI that you must track is how much it costs you to get a lead. A lead is any person who has inquired about your business either by phone, internet or by visiting.

> " *The first marketing KPI that you must track is how much it costs you to get a lead.*

Let's suppose that you ran an ad in your local newspaper. It cost you $400 to run the ad. You obtained 5 phone calls, 4 internet leads and 9 people came in to either get information or try out a class. This means that the total number of people who responded to your ad was 18. By dividing the total number of responses into your total marketing spend you get an average "lead acquisition cost" of $22.22.

Tracking your lead acquisition cost is important because it helps you determine whether or not your advertising was worthwhile. Furthermore, when you combine the LAC with the next number, "customer acquisition cost," you have important information regarding how well you are converting prospects into students. For example, if you get 18 people to respond to an ad but only 5 ultimately become regular members, your conversion rate would be just 27%. Such a low conversion rate would indicate that a problem exists in some part of product delivery (classes not meeting their schedule, type of classes not right, don't like the physical facility, don't like the instructor, etc.).

CUSTOMER ACQUISITION COST (CAC)

The next marketing KPI is customer acquisition cost. This refers to how much it actually cost you to obtain a new student. To determine this number you simply take the total number of people who actually became a member as a result of a particular marketing effort and divide it by the actual dollars spent. In our earlier example we had 18 prospects contact us from an ad in the newspaper. If only 5 became regular students (remember the ad cost $400) then the CAC from that marketing effort would be $80.

For those of you new to KPI's you may be thinking, "Wow, $80 to get a new student that seems expensive." Our response to that is, "It depends." If the lifetime value of a customer was $1,500 then spending $80 to get the customer isn't at all expensive. In fact, that would represent a marketing cost of around 5%, which is very low. So, as you can see, all your business decisions must be analyzed and made by looking at the numbers—all the numbers.

HOW TO TRACK

Once you understand and appreciate the importance of KPI's, the next logical question is, "How the heck do I track all these numbers?" In order to track your KPI's you have to be collecting them on a daily basis. That may sound obvious but very often in the business of yoga classes and studios there is a reliance on paper sign-ins and, in most cases, no front desk sign in process. This relaxed type environment often makes for poor tracking of numbers, hence the inability to really know your KPI's.

The only way that you are going to be able to track all these numbers is with a computer software program. Certainly you could be tracking things manually (like class attendance) and then inputting that information into some kind of customized excel program but that will be an administrative nightmare. You really need to consider the time it will take to get sub-par data and compare that to the small investment most online software portals are.

> " *Software programs that are specifically designed for yoga studios are called member management systems.*

Software programs that are specifically designed for yoga studios are called member management systems. Perhaps the most popular for yoga studios is www.mindbodyonline.com. This company is also very popular in the health club business as well. There are others too. www.zenplanner.com, www.perfectmind. com and www.paysimple.com. Certainly you need to spend some time with each, determining if it is a fit for your business AND assess it as it relates to an auto responder program. It is important to note that some member management software programs have good contact management systems while others do not. When assessing which to invest in, use the checklist we provided you with back in the chapter on Contact Management systems to make the right selection.

CHAPTER 13
CONCLUSION

We have covered a lot of information in this book. In actuality this publication is more like a reference than simply a book. You literally could keep it on your desk and refer to one section every day as a checklist for successfully running your yoga studio or classes. We realize that for many, a lot of the information discussed is new and can be overwhelming. Our suggestion is to go back through the book, chapter by chapter, and simply work through the materials without judgments. It doesn't matter if you are currently doing none of these things or most of them. The goal is to help you become more successful at the business of yoga. By helping you attain greater financial success it will free you up to do more of what you love—teaching.

We wish you much success with your business and hope to hear about how you have implemented the strategies and ideas contained in this book.

HELP DEEPEN YOUR STUDENTS PRACTICE & GENERATE ADDITIONAL REVENUE

Essential oils have been used in the practice of yoga for centuries. Just as ever post corresponds with each of the chakras, certain essential oils support specific chakras. In addition, the aromas of essential oils influence the brain emotionally and spiritually. Finally, specific essential oils help alleviate muscle aches and pains and can aid in faster post class recovery.

Instructors and studios that incorporate essential oils into their classes discover that their students can deepen their practice, reduce fatigue and injury and often establish a stronger connection to the instructor or studio aiding in attendance.

If you are interested in learning more about essential oils and yoga, please go to www.letsdoyoga.com/yogabusiness to receive our free eBooklet. Included is a guide for choosing the best essential oils and specific ways to incorporate them as a revenue generator for your business.

ABOUT THE AUTHORS

Casey Conrad has been in the health and fitness industry for over 27 years. She is the President of Communication Consultants, a company dedicated to providing high quality sales, marketing and management seminars for professionals in the health and fitness industry worldwide. www. HealthClubSalesTraining.com .

In addition to authoring "Selling Fitness: The Complete Guide to Selling Health Club Memberships," she has created and published over 24 other sales and marketing products specifically for the health and fitness industry, including "Selling Personal Training" and her most recent "Internet Marketing for Health & Fitness Clubs." www.SmartClubMarketing.com

Casey is also the creator of the in-club weight loss-licensing program called Take It Off that provides clubs with a simple weight loss solution for their members while adding a valuable ancillary revenue stream. www.TakeItOffWeightLoss.com .

In 2000 Casey founded Healthy Inspirations, an international chain of women's weight loss and fitness centers. She was responsible for creating all the sales training programs and marketing materials for the entire organization, which reached 122 locations before she sold out in 2008.

She has been a featured presenter in 20 countries, and has spoken for numerous health club industry organizations including IHRSA, Club Industry, Network for Fitness Professionals in Australia, Gold's Gym Enterprises, Bodylife in England and Germany, Forum in Italy, EFFA in Holland and Asiafit in Hong Kong and Beijing. In addition, Casey is a featured columnist for numerous health club industry magazines and publications.

She received her BA from The American University and her JD at Roger Williams University School of Law.

Howard VanEs, M.A., E-RYT 500 has been committed to wellness and fitness for over 28 years. He has a deep passion for helping people learn about the many ways they can improve the quality of their health and lives through mind/body methods.

For over 23 years, Howard has been a dedicated practitioner of hatha yoga and has been teaching yoga for the last 18 years in the Bay area of California. Howard has written many yoga related books, as well as numerous others focused on health and wellness.

His books include:

- *Yoga: The Back Pain Cure. The Yoga Therapy Back Care and Low Back Pain Treatment Program*

- *Beginning Yoga: A Practice Manual.*

- *ABS! 50 of the Best core exercises to strengthen, tone, and flatten your belly.*

- *Meditation: The Gift Inside. How to meditate to quiet your mind, find inner peace, and lasting happiness!*

- *Ageless Beauty & Timeless Strength: A woman's guide to building upper body strength without any special equipment.*

In addition to writing about and teaching yoga, Howard also leads yoga teacher trainings and wellness seminars and retreats worldwide.

Howard received a yoga teacher certification from Mt. Madonna Center in Watsonville, CA and has also received training from the advanced studies program at The Iyengar Institute of San Francisco. Prior to becoming a yoga instructor Howard owned an award winning advertising agency. He also has an M.A. in counseling psychology.

His websites are www.letsdoyoga.com and www.booksonhealth.net.